French Revolution Step by Step

The Forces and Faces Behind Historic Uprisings & Reforms

Jack Davidson

© 2024 by Jack Davidson

All rights reserved.

No part of this publication may be reproduced, distributed, or transmitted in any form or by any means, including photocopying, recording, or other electronic or mechanical methods, without the prior written permission of the publisher, except in the case of brief quotations embodied in critical reviews and certain other noncommercial uses permitted by U.S. copyright law.

This book is intended to provide general information on the subjects covered and is presented with the understanding that the author and publisher are not providing professional advice or services. While every effort has been made to ensure the accuracy and completeness of the information contained herein, neither the author nor the publisher guarantees such accuracy or completeness, nor shall they be responsible for any errors or omissions or for the results obtained from the use of such information. The contents of this book are provided "as is" and without warranties of any kind, either express or implied.

Publisher email: info@tagvault.org

PREFACE

The French Revolution remains one of the most significant and complex periods in history, marking the profound transformation of an entire society. This movement sparked widespread change, not only in France but around the world. It's a story of ambition, desperation, bravery, and the human yearning for a better life. It's also a story of conflict, bloodshed, and, ultimately, the triumph of revolutionary ideas. *French Revolution Step by Step - From Monarchy to Republic: Unraveling the Causes, Chaos, and Consequences* invites you on a journey through these tumultuous years to explore how and why this transformation occurred.

The French Revolution began in 1789, triggered by a combination of social, economic, and political factors that had been building for decades. France was a country divided by deep social inequality, with a vast majority of its population living in poverty and facing heavy taxation, while a privileged few enjoyed lives of wealth and influence. Compounded by economic crisis, royal corruption, and the influence of Enlightenment ideas promoting freedom and equality, a powerful desire for change swept through the people of France.

But the Revolution was much more than the simple overthrow of a king and queen. It was a complex series of events, each building on the last, filled with shifting alliances, competing ideologies, and passionate debates about what a just society should look like. This book begins with the "Seeds of Discontent," a chapter dedicated to the underlying issues that set the stage for revolution. Each chapter that follows details key moments and movements, introducing important figures and exploring their actions, ideas, and the consequences of their choices.

We continue through some of the Revolution's most dramatic moments, like the meeting of the Estates-General, the storming of the Bastille, and the drafting of the Declaration of the Rights of Man and Citizen. We'll go into the power struggles within the newly formed National Assembly and the deep divisions that emerged among revolutionaries. From political debates to armed conflicts, from the Reign of Terror to the eventual rise of Napoleon, every chapter is designed to give you a clear and accessible understanding of this chaotic and fascinating era.

While the French Revolution marked a break from the past, it was also an origin point for many modern ideals that are central to our lives today. Ideas like equality before the law, freedom of speech, and democratic representation trace back to this period. Throughout the book, you'll find these themes discussed, showing how the debates of the Revolution were a first step toward shaping ideas that continue to guide societies worldwide.

Each chapter is broken into manageable sections, with subtopics that help simplify complex events and themes. We also highlight key figures like Marie Antoinette,

Robespierre, and Napoleon, exploring their roles in both moving the Revolution forward and shaping its eventual outcomes. You'll meet the unsung heroes—the women, peasants, and lesser-known revolutionaries—who fought tirelessly for a new order, demanding to be heard in a society that had long ignored them.

Toward the end of this book, we'll explore the Revolution's legacy, analyzing how it inspired future movements for freedom and justice and its impact on world history. Finally, for easy reference, we've included a timeline that maps out the Revolution's key moments and a glossary that defines essential terms. This structure makes it simple for you to follow the Revolution step by step, from its roots in royal France to its ripple effects that resonate even today.

In writing this book, my aim was to create a guide that is comprehensive yet accessible, informative but engaging. History can sometimes seem distant and complex, but in understanding events like the French Revolution, we gain insight into the human condition itself. What drove the French people to take up arms against their king? What inspired them to demand freedom and equality, even in the face of great danger? These are questions that have fascinated scholars for centuries, and I hope this book helps you find your own answers.

Whether you are new to studying the French Revolution or have some knowledge already, this book is designed to be approachable. By breaking down the Revolution's causes, chaos, and consequences, my hope is that it offers you a clear and memorable understanding of how this moment changed France and, ultimately, the world.

Thank you for joining me on this journey into the French Revolution. Let's step back into history and discover together the events that transformed a nation and inspired generations to come.

TOPICAL OUTLINE

Chapter 1: Seeds of Discontent
- The Ancien Régime
- Economic Strains and Financial Crisis
- Social Inequality and the Estates System
- Enlightenment Ideals and Philosophers
- Corruption and Inefficiency in Government
- Influence of the American Revolution
- Early Revolutionary Sentiments and Movements

Chapter 2: The Meeting of the Estates-General
- The Calling of the Estates-General
- Tensions Between the Estates
- The Rise of the Third Estate

Chapter 3: The Tennis Court Oath and Formation of the National Assembly
- The Significance of the Tennis Court Oath
- Creation of the National Assembly
- The Declaration of Intent for Change
- The Role of Key Leaders

Chapter 4: Storming the Bastille
- Symbolism of the Bastille
- Events Leading to the Storming
- Aftermath and Public Response

Chapter 5: The Great Fear and Rural Revolts
- Peasant Uprisings and Rebellion
- Spread of Fear and Panic Across France
- Rural Revolts and Attack on Feudal Symbols

Chapter 6: Abolition of Feudal Privileges
- The August Decrees
- End of Noble Privileges and Feudal Rights
- Response from the Aristocracy and Clergy

Chapter 7: The Declaration of the Rights of Man and Citizen
- Drafting and Ideals of the Declaration
- Influence of Enlightenment Thought
- Key Rights and Freedoms Established

- Global Influence of the Declaration

Chapter 8: Women in the Revolution
- Women's March on Versailles
- Role of Women's Societies and Clubs
- Revolutionary Women Leaders
- Struggles for Rights and Recognition

Chapter 9: Reforms and Reorganization of France
- Economic and Tax Reforms
- Church and State Separation (Civil Constitution of the Clergy)
- Administrative and Legal Changes

Chapter 10: The Rise of Factions and Political Clubs
- Emergence of the Jacobins, Girondins, and Others
- Debates on Governance and Policies
- The Role of Public Opinion and Political Clubs

Chapter 11: War with Neighboring Monarchies
- Causes of the Revolutionary Wars
- Early Battles and Mobilization
- Internal Opposition and Foreign Threats

Chapter 12: The Reign of Terror
- Rise of the Committee of Public Safety
- Role of Robespierre and Radical Leadership
- Policies of Terror and Purges

Chapter 13: The Fall of Robespierre and End of Terror
- Growing Opposition to Robespierre
- Key Events Leading to His Arrest
- Impact of the Fall and End of Terror

Chapter 14: The Thermidorian Reaction and Directory Era
- Reforms and Reaction Against Extremism
- Establishment of the Directory
- Challenges Facing the New Government

Chapter 15: The Rise of Napoleon and the End of the Revolution
- Military Success and Popularity of Napoleon
- Overthrow of the Directory

- Establishment of the Consulate and End of Revolutionary France

Chapter 16: Legacy of the French Revolution
- Social and Political Impact on France
- Influence on Global Revolutionary Movements
- Lasting Effects on Modern Ideals of Equality, Rights, and Governance

Chapter 17: Timeline and Terms
- Timeline
- Terms and Definitions

Afterword

TABLE OF CONTENTS

Chapter 1: Seeds of Discontent ... 1
Chapter 2: The Meeting of the Estates-General ... 22
Chapter 3: The Tennis Court Oath and Formation of the National Assembly ... 29
Chapter 4: Storming the Bastille ... 38
Chapter 5: The Great Fear and Rural Revolts ... 45
Chapter 6: Abolition of Feudal Privileges ... 52
Chapter 7: The Declaration of the Rights of Man and Citizen ... 58
Chapter 8: Women in the Revolution ... 66
Chapter 9: Reforms and Reorganization of France ... 74
Chapter 10: The Rise of Factions and Political Clubs ... 79
Chapter 11: War with Neighboring Monarchies ... 86
Chapter 12: The Reign of Terror ... 92
Chapter 13: The Fall of Robespierre and End of Terror ... 99
Chapter 14: The Thermidorian Reaction and Directory Era ... 104
Chapter 15: The Rise of Napoleon and the End of the Revolution ... 110
Chapter 16: Legacy of the French Revolution ... 115
Chapter 17: Timeline and Terms ... 121
Afterword ... 128

CHAPTER 1: SEEDS OF DISCONTENT

The Ancien Régime

The Ancien Régime was the deeply entrenched social, political, and economic system that defined France before the Revolution. For centuries, it structured French society in a rigid hierarchy, upholding strict roles and privileges. The very term "Ancien Régime"—literally meaning "old rule"—reflects a system rooted in monarchy, nobility, and religion, which collectively dictated the lives of the French people, from peasants to aristocrats. Understanding the Ancien Régime is essential to grasping why the French Revolution erupted so explosively in 1789.

In the Ancien Régime, **France operated as an absolute monarchy**. At its peak stood the king, who wielded immense control over the government, military, and judicial systems. French kings, particularly those of the Bourbon dynasty, governed with near-complete autonomy, claiming divine right as the source of their power. This divine right concept was more than a mere statement; it was an unspoken social contract that justified the king's authority as being sanctioned by God. Louis XIV, known as the "Sun King," took this idea further, famously proclaiming, "L'état, c'est moi" ("I am the state"). He transformed the monarchy into a centralized and opulent institution, centered around Versailles, which became both a physical and symbolic manifestation of royal power. Later kings, however, lacked Louis XIV's vision and authority. By the time Louis XVI came to the throne, the monarchy faced severe disapproval. Louis XVI's hesitancy, coupled with his failure to respond effectively to crises, eroded the reverence once held for the monarchy, leaving a society primed for rebellion.

Below the king sat the nobility, who held significant privileges and responsibilities. This aristocratic class was divided into two primary groups: the **nobles of the sword** and the **nobles of the robe**. The nobles of the sword traced their lineage back to medieval warrior nobility and held traditional rights over land and peasantry. They enjoyed feudal privileges that granted them control over local governance and military power, often without paying taxes. In contrast, the nobles of the robe gained their status through royal appointments or purchased titles, especially positions within the legal and administrative apparatus. These nobles often served as judges, magistrates, and bureaucrats, filling crucial roles in the complex web of France's administrative system. Despite their differences, both groups of nobles enjoyed special legal privileges, exempt from many taxes and dues that burdened ordinary citizens.

While nobles thrived, the **commoners, or Third Estate**, comprised the vast majority of France's population. The Third Estate was diverse, including wealthy merchants, small shopkeepers, artisans, and the vast rural peasantry. The wealthier members of this estate, known as the bourgeoisie, had increasingly accumulated financial power through commerce and trade, particularly in cities like Paris, Lyon, and Bordeaux. These bourgeois families often aspired to elevate their social standing and resented their exclusion from the privileges enjoyed by the nobility. Many of them read Enlightenment thinkers like Rousseau, Voltaire, and Montesquieu, who argued for reason, secularism, and governance reform. The intellectual ferment provided bourgeois families with the ideological tools to critique the Ancien Régime, feeding their growing discontent.

For the **peasantry**, life was harsh and unforgiving under the Ancien Régime. Peasants labored on land they rarely owned, paying rents to landowners and taxes to the king. They faced obligations such as the **tithe**, a tax to the Catholic Church, which required them to give a portion of their crops or earnings. This tax was particularly resented because it represented an economic drain that provided little benefit in return. Many peasants lived on subsistence agriculture, barely growing enough to survive, especially when harvests were poor. Unlike the nobility, who were largely exempt, peasants bore the heaviest burden of **direct taxes**, such as the taille, a property tax, and the gabelle, a salt tax. The high tax burden, coupled with minimal protections from legal abuses, meant that peasants lived in a state of near-constant vulnerability and insecurity.

The **Catholic Church** was influential in the Ancien Régime, acting as a religious, social, and political pillar. The Church controlled significant portions of land across France, especially in rural areas, where it was often the largest landowner. This land ownership not only gave the Church wealth but also considerable influence over local affairs. Bishops, who were frequently noble-born, enjoyed substantial power and privileges. The Church, as a pillar of the monarchy, reinforced loyalty to the king and to the social order. Through religious teachings and sermons, it promoted obedience, humility, and acceptance of social hierarchies. However, while the Church's wealth and power were widely known, its close ties to the monarchy and the aristocracy bred resentment among the commoners, who saw the clergy as indifferent to their suffering. Furthermore, the Church's authority meant it could censor books, prohibit gatherings, and restrict the spread of Enlightenment ideas, adding to its unpopularity in the lead-up to the Revolution.

Economically, the Ancien Régime suffered from outdated and rigid systems that could not adapt to France's changing society. The economy was predominantly agrarian, heavily reliant on peasant labor. Despite pockets of wealth generated through trade and colonial ventures, France's economy remained vulnerable. Successive kings, including Louis XIV and Louis XV, plunged France into debt with costly wars, including the War of the Spanish Succession and the Seven Years' War. This accumulation of debt created a fiscal crisis that burdened subsequent administrations. To fund the state, the monarchy increasingly relied on borrowing, creating an unsustainable situation in which France could barely afford to pay the interest on its loans. Efforts to reform this system met fierce resistance from the nobility, who opposed any measures that would erode their tax exemptions.

Compounding these economic woes were **periodic food shortages** and famines that devastated the lower classes. France's agricultural economy was extremely vulnerable to climatic fluctuations, with bad harvests leading directly to food scarcity. When harvests failed, bread prices soared, and bread was the main staple for most of the population. The bread crisis of the 1780s, exacerbated by a poor harvest in 1788, drove food prices to levels that impoverished families could not afford. Starvation and malnutrition became widespread, and discontent grew. Bread riots erupted in many regions, leading to increased animosity toward the ruling classes. The fact that the nobility and clergy continued their extravagant lifestyles, despite the suffering around them, amplified the perception of the Ancien Régime as unjust and out of touch.

The political structure of the Ancien Régime was chaotic and fragmented. France was divided into a complex system of provinces, each with its own laws, customs, and forms of taxation. This made governance difficult and fueled resentment, as the laws and taxes varied significantly between regions. Furthermore, France lacked a central assembly or parliament with the power to legislate for the whole country. Although a central court system existed, known as the Parlement, it was more of a judicial body than a legislative one. Attempts to reform the legal and administrative systems were sporadic and often blocked by powerful noble interests. Without a central, representative body to address the concerns of the people, voices demanding change grew louder.

The Enlightenment, with its rational and secular ideas, directly challenged the foundation of the Ancien Régime. Enlightenment thinkers argued that authority should derive from reason and the consent of the governed rather than divine right or hereditary privilege. The philosophes, as Enlightenment writers were known, condemned the injustices of the Ancien Régime and advocated for equality before the law, individual rights, and separation of powers. These ideas resonated especially with the educated bourgeoisie, who found them useful in critiquing a system they perceived as corrupt and self-serving. As Enlightenment texts circulated in cafés, salons, and private homes, they planted seeds of radical thought, influencing not only intellectuals but also common citizens. Works like Rousseau's *The Social Contract* and Montesquieu's *The Spirit of the Laws* inspired readers to question why they should accept a system that served only a minority at the top.

In 1787, the government's need for financial reform reached a breaking point. Louis XVI, pressured by advisors, called an Assembly of Notables—an extraordinary gathering of nobles, clergy, and other elite figures—to address the financial crisis. However, this assembly refused to approve any new taxes or reforms, arguing that only the Estates-General, a larger representative body that hadn't convened since 1614, held the authority to do so. This resistance revealed the depth of the monarchy's crisis. Without the support of the nobility, the king's authority weakened, while calls for a wider meeting grew louder. When the Estates-General was finally called in 1789, it marked the beginning of a series of events that would dismantle the Ancien Régime.

The Ancien Régime represented a system stretched to its limits, held together by tradition, privilege, and divine right. Yet by the 1780s, its flaws had become too apparent and too oppressive for many French people to ignore. France had grown more complex and interconnected, while the Ancien Régime remained rigid and resistant to change. In attempting to preserve its traditional structures, it sowed the seeds of its own collapse.

Economic Strains and Financial Crisis

The economic strains facing France in the years leading up to the Revolution were immense. The financial crisis didn't arise suddenly; it was the result of years of costly wars, ineffective tax systems, and unchecked government spending that drained the state's resources. France's **financial problems** were among the primary triggers that pushed the nation toward revolution, exposing the weaknesses of the Ancien Régime and highlighting the desperate need for reform.

By the late 1700s, **France's national debt** was staggering, driven by repeated wars and lavish spending. Louis XIV's long and costly reign had already left France in deep debt by the time Louis XV ascended the throne. Louis XV's own reign continued in the same vein, with expenditures on wars, including the War of the Austrian Succession and the Seven Years' War, only adding to the already enormous debt. By the time Louis XVI became king in 1774, France's financial condition was dire, with a significant portion of its annual budget consumed solely by interest payments on loans. The debt grew to a point where nearly 50 percent of state revenue was used to service it, meaning funds meant for other critical functions, like infrastructure or national defense, were largely diverted toward paying creditors.

One of the critical issues in France's financial structure was its **ineffective and highly unequal tax system**. French society was divided into three main estates, with each group taxed differently, creating an imbalanced system that worsened the economic crisis. The First Estate (the clergy) and the Second Estate (the nobility) enjoyed various exemptions from direct taxes, which fell mainly on the Third Estate. This Third Estate was made up of peasants, urban workers, and the bourgeoisie, the latter being a growing class of wealthy merchants, professionals, and intellectuals. Despite their different levels of wealth, nearly all members of the Third Estate shouldered the main tax burdens, from the taille (a property tax) to the gabelle (a tax on salt). Meanwhile, the privileged classes, especially the nobility, resisted reforms to broaden the tax base, insisting on their traditional exemptions.

The tax system's inefficiency ran deeper than who was taxed. **Collecting taxes in France was a disorganized and corrupt process.** In many cases, the state did not collect taxes directly. Instead, it relied on a network of private tax farmers, individuals or companies contracted to collect taxes on behalf of the crown. Tax farmers were notorious for exploiting their positions, often charging more than the official rate and keeping the difference as profit. The system of **"ferme générale"** (tax farming) not only led to widespread corruption but also meant that a significant amount of revenue never reached the royal treasury. Additionally, certain regions of France enjoyed special tax privileges, with local authorities negotiating favorable terms for themselves. As a result, the total tax revenue fell short of what was needed to address the state's expenses.

Compounding the financial crisis was the **high cost of the American Revolutionary War**. In 1778, France entered the war on the side of the American colonies against Britain. French leaders saw it as an opportunity to weaken their old enemy and reclaim some lost pride after the defeat in the Seven Years' War. However, supporting the American colonists came at a significant price. Financing the war meant additional borrowing, and by its end in 1783, France had accumulated another substantial debt. This added financial strain came with little tangible benefit to the French people. To many in France, it seemed that the government was willing to spend vast amounts of money on a distant conflict while ignoring the needs of its own citizens, deepening frustration and distrust.

Economic mismanagement further worsened the crisis. Many of the financial ministers under Louis XVI attempted reforms to stabilize the economy, yet they faced resistance from the nobility and the king himself. One prominent finance minister, **Jacques Necker**, proposed various measures to address the debt, including cutting government expenses and instituting some tax reforms. Necker also took the unusual step of publishing a budget, the *Compte rendu au roi*, which provided some transparency to the public. However, Necker's budget overstated France's financial health, leading people to believe the situation was less dire than it was. His other attempts to reduce privileges and broaden the tax base met resistance from the nobility, and he was ultimately dismissed. His successors, including Charles Alexandre de Calonne, faced similar struggles. Calonne attempted a broader set of reforms, including a universal land tax that would apply to all estates, but opposition from the nobility halted these efforts as well.

One of the worst aspects of the economic crisis was its **impact on food prices and living conditions for the common people**. France was heavily agrarian, with the majority of its population relying on agriculture for survival. When agricultural production faltered, as it did repeatedly in the years leading up to the Revolution, the entire economy suffered. Poor harvests in the late 1780s created food shortages, which led to drastic increases in the price of bread. Bread was the staple food for most people in France, and when prices rose, ordinary families faced the very real threat of starvation. In the harsh winter of 1788-1789, a series of severe frost events further reduced food supplies, pushing prices even higher and sparking widespread unrest.

With food prices soaring, the urban poor and rural peasants alike **faced extreme hardships**. Hunger drove people to the brink, with bread riots breaking out in various towns. These riots were often led by women, who bore the brunt of feeding their families and felt the strain of rising costs directly. Crowds would storm bakeries or grain stores, demanding fair prices or seizing food by force. The government, unable to address the people's grievances and seen as indifferent or inept, lost legitimacy in the eyes of the public. The perception that the monarchy was unwilling or unable to address basic needs heightened social tensions, creating an atmosphere ripe for revolution.

The government's desperate need for revenue led it to impose even harsher demands on the Third Estate. Despite their already heavy tax burden, commoners were often subjected to additional levies and forced contributions. These financial demands went beyond mere taxes. Many peasants were required to perform labor services, known as the **corvée**, where they worked on public projects like road construction without pay. These obligations added to the resentment of the lower classes, who felt they were bearing the weight of the state's financial failures without any benefit.

As financial reform stalled, **Louis XVI's government became increasingly unstable**. By the late 1780s, with debt spiraling and public discontent growing, the king's advisors recognized that the existing system could no longer sustain itself. In an attempt to gain support for new taxes, Louis XVI called an Assembly of Notables in 1787. This group consisted of influential nobles and clergy, who were asked to approve tax reforms, but they refused, insisting that only the Estates-General had the authority to pass new taxes. The refusal of the nobility to accept even modest reforms demonstrated their determination to preserve their privileges at the expense of the general population.

In the end, the mounting financial crisis forced Louis XVI to convene the **Estates-General** in May 1789. This assembly, which had not been called since 1614, was a pivotal moment in the lead-up to the Revolution. It signaled the king's acknowledgment of the government's inability to solve the crisis through traditional means. The Estates-General brought representatives from all three estates together to discuss potential solutions to the kingdom's problems, including the financial crisis. However, tensions within the assembly quickly arose, as members of the Third Estate, who represented the common people, demanded greater representation and influence.

Ultimately, the **economic strains and financial crisis** of the Ancien Régime exposed the fundamental weaknesses of the monarchy and the nobility. These strains revealed a system that privileged a small elite at the expense of the broader population. Despite repeated warnings and numerous opportunities to reform, the monarchy's inability to adapt and address these financial problems contributed directly to the Revolution. The refusal of the privileged estates to share the burden of taxation and the government's failure to address the immediate needs of its people set the stage for a dramatic reshaping of French society.

The Ancien Régime, already teetering under centuries-old structures, could not withstand the pressures of a modernizing economy, growing public awareness, and widespread dissatisfaction. When the French people looked around and saw no hope of relief under the current system, they were ready for revolutionary change.

Social Inequality and the Estates System

Let's look at the **Estates System** is more depth. This was a rigid social hierarchy that defined life in pre-revolutionary France. It divided people into three distinct social classes, or "Estates," each with specific rights, privileges, and duties. This structure was not just a social system; it was a system of governance that shaped how people worked, lived, and interacted with one another. In a society where each person's place was legally defined, this system enforced clear separations between social classes and left little opportunity for mobility. The Estates System fueled frustration and resentment that ultimately ignited the French Revolution.

At the top of this hierarchy was the **First Estate**, made up of the **clergy**. The Church held enormous influence, not only as a religious institution but as a political and economic power. Clergy members were exempt from most taxes and instead imposed a tithe on the population, a kind of religious tax that required the faithful to contribute a portion of their income or crops. This tithe provided the Church with a steady flow of resources, making it one of the wealthiest institutions in France. The Church owned around 10 percent of the land, which it leased to peasants and others for cultivation. It also maintained its own courts and legal privileges, operating as a largely autonomous institution within the state. While the Church performed social services, such as education and care for the poor, its wealth and privileges made it an object of public resentment, particularly among those who bore the burden of taxes that the clergy were exempt from.

Beneath the clergy was the **Second Estate**, which consisted of the **nobility**. Like the clergy, the nobles enjoyed vast privileges and exemptions from taxes. The nobility was divided into two main groups: the "nobles of the sword" and the "nobles of the robe." Nobles of the sword traced their status back to medieval times and often held traditional roles in the military. Nobles of the robe, on the other hand, had acquired their titles more recently, usually through service in administrative or legal positions, often purchased from the monarchy itself. Nobles held prominent roles in government, the military, and the court, and they controlled significant portions of land across the country. They, too, were exempt from most taxes, including the taille, the principal land tax that commoners paid. Instead, nobles collected **feudal dues** from the peasants who lived and worked on their land. These dues could be taxes, labor, or other obligations, reinforcing the dependency of the lower classes on their landlords. This privileged status, paired with their resistance to reform, made the nobility a symbol of inequality in the eyes of the Third Estate.

At the bottom of this hierarchy sat the **Third Estate**, encompassing the vast majority of France's population. The Third Estate was diverse, including wealthy and educated bourgeoisie, skilled artisans, urban workers, and the rural peasantry. Despite their different social and economic conditions, everyone in the Third Estate shared one characteristic: they had few rights and little political influence. They were subject to nearly all of the taxes from which the First and Second Estates were exempt, including the taille, the gabelle (a salt tax), and the corvée (a labor tax). The **bourgeoisie**, the wealthier, educated members of the Third Estate, often had significant economic power and influence within cities. These merchants, lawyers, and intellectuals wanted more say in government, as they saw themselves as key players in the economy. Many bourgeois were influenced by Enlightenment ideas, which promoted equality, reason, and the rejection of inherited privilege. However, despite their wealth and education, they remained excluded from positions of political power, which were reserved for the nobility and the clergy.

Most of the **Third Estate** were not affluent bourgeois, but rather peasants who worked the land. The life of a peasant was harsh and unforgiving. Peasants faced a constant struggle to survive, working long hours on land they did not own and paying various dues to both the nobility and the Church. They owed feudal dues to their landlords, paid the tithe to the Church, and were subject to the king's taxes. Additionally, they were required to perform the **corvée**, a form of unpaid labor for public projects, such as road repair. The corvée was especially resented, as it took time and energy that could have been used for their own livelihoods. These burdens left many peasants in perpetual poverty, with little hope of improving their circumstances. Peasants also had little recourse to justice; local lords often held judicial powers, and disputes were resolved in seigneurial courts that were biased toward the nobility. The frustrations of this class, facing high taxes and near-impossible demands, contributed significantly to the discontent that erupted in 1789.

The urban poor, or **sans-culottes**, made up another segment of the Third Estate. These individuals included day laborers, artisans, and other low-wage workers in cities like Paris. Unlike peasants, who could grow their own food, the sans-culottes relied on purchasing their provisions, particularly bread. Any fluctuation in the price of bread could be devastating. When bread prices rose due to poor harvests or economic mismanagement, the sans-culottes often faced starvation. They were among the most politically radical groups in the Revolution, participating in protests and riots and pushing for reforms that went beyond what the bourgeoisie envisioned. Their desperation and hunger made them a volatile and vocal force, adding to the revolutionary fervor sweeping the country.

One of the defining aspects of the **Estates System** was its **legal and social rigidity**. Social mobility was almost impossible. Birth largely determined a person's role in society. While some bourgeois could purchase titles or marry into the nobility, these cases were rare and did little to alter the overall structure. The nobility jealously guarded its status, often going to great lengths to prevent commoners from entering their ranks. Even in government, access to positions of power was tightly controlled. Most positions were filled through patronage, inheritance, or purchase, ensuring that power remained within the upper estates.

The **Estates-General**, the closest thing France had to a national assembly, reflected this structure and inequality. The Estates-General included representatives from all three estates, but voting was done by estate rather than by individual, meaning each estate cast one vote. This system effectively neutralized the Third Estate, which represented the vast majority of the population. The First and Second Estates could vote together, outnumbering the Third Estate despite their smaller numbers. When Louis XVI called the Estates-General in 1789 to address the financial crisis, the Third Estate demanded that voting be based on headcount, giving them a fairer representation. This demand marked one of the earliest confrontations in the Revolution and highlighted the frustration of the Third Estate at being politically marginalized.

The Estates System did more than enforce inequality; it **created resentment and division**. The First and Second Estates benefited directly from the labor, taxes, and resources of the Third Estate without contributing equally. They enjoyed privileges that commoners could never hope to attain. This disparity was glaringly apparent, especially in rural areas where peasants labored under landlords who often lived far away, reaping the rewards of the land without witnessing the hardship of those who worked it. In cities, the sight of nobles living in luxury while workers struggled to afford bread only added to the bitterness. The sense of injustice permeated every level of society, fueling a desire for change.

The influence of **Enlightenment thinkers** further exacerbated these tensions. Writers like Rousseau, Voltaire, and Montesquieu challenged the notion of inherited privilege and promoted ideas of equality and individual rights. Their ideas found a receptive audience among the bourgeoisie, who saw in them a rationale for their own frustrations with the existing order. The Enlightenment presented an intellectual framework that questioned the legitimacy of a system where privilege was based on birth rather than merit. These ideas trickled down to other segments of the Third Estate, creating a population increasingly aware of the injustices they faced. As they read or heard about Enlightenment ideals, members of the Third Estate began to imagine an alternative to the Estates System—a society where they might have a voice, a chance to shape their own futures.

Ultimately, the Estates System bound French society in an outdated and deeply unfair structure. It allowed a small minority to thrive while the vast majority struggled under heavy burdens. The Third Estate's resentment grew as they realized that the existing system offered no hope of improvement. The rigid barriers between the estates created a society divided not just by wealth, but by opportunity and dignity. When the Revolution began, one of its primary aims was to dismantle these artificial divisions and to create a society where merit and equality would replace privilege and birthright. The Estates System, with its layers of privilege and oppression, was not just a structure; it was a symbol of everything the Revolution aimed to destroy.

Enlightenment Ideals and Philosophers

The **Enlightenment** was a powerful intellectual movement that spread across Europe in the 18th century. Its ideas deeply influenced the French Revolution, planting the seeds of discontent with the established order and inspiring a vision of a new, fairer society. The Enlightenment challenged traditional sources of authority—especially monarchy and religion—and promoted values like reason, equality, and individual rights. In France, **philosophers** known as *philosophes* spread these revolutionary ideas through books, pamphlets, and public debates, stirring up critical questions about justice, governance, and the purpose of government itself.

One of the most influential figures of the Enlightenment was **Jean-Jacques Rousseau**. In his famous work *The Social Contract*, published in 1762, Rousseau proposed that society should be based on a "social contract" between its members rather than on traditional hierarchies of birth and privilege. Rousseau argued that legitimate political authority comes from the consent of the governed, not from divine right or inherited power. This idea was revolutionary. Rousseau believed that in a fair society, people must agree to rules that serve the common good, and he emphasized the concept of the "general will"—the collective interest of the people. For Rousseau, the purpose of government was to serve this general will and protect equality and freedom. His ideas offered a sharp contrast to the authoritarian structure of the Ancien Régime, where the king's will was considered absolute.

Rousseau also argued that **inequality** was an unnatural condition. In *Discourse on the Origin and Basis of Inequality Among Men*, he explained that social inequalities were created by man, not nature. He suggested that society had corrupted the natural goodness of humans by imposing artificial distinctions based on wealth, birth, and rank. These ideas resonated deeply with the Third Estate, especially the bourgeoisie, who felt shut out of positions of power by the aristocracy. Rousseau's work inspired many revolutionary leaders, who cited his ideas as they called for an end to the feudal privileges of the nobility and the creation of a society based on equality and justice.

Voltaire, another towering figure of the Enlightenment, took a different approach to critique society. Known for his wit and sharp criticism, Voltaire was relentless in his attacks on the Catholic Church and the monarchy. In his writings, he condemned **religious intolerance, censorship, and the abuses of power** by the clergy and nobility. Voltaire did not argue for democracy; he believed in enlightened despotism, where a ruler governed in the best interests of the people. However, he passionately advocated for **freedom of speech, freedom of thought, and separation of church and state**. In his view, these freedoms were essential for a rational and just society.

Voltaire's influence was particularly strong among educated members of the Third Estate, who shared his frustration with the Church's influence over public life. The Church, as part of the First Estate, wielded significant power in France, not only as a spiritual institution but as a landowner and economic force. Voltaire criticized this dual role, arguing that it corrupted the Church's mission and allowed it to exploit the people. He famously said, "Écrasez l'infâme" ("Crush the infamous thing"), referring to what he saw as the corrupt and oppressive elements of the Church. His call for secular governance and individual freedoms resonated deeply with those who felt trapped by the rigid hierarchy of the Ancien Régime.

Montesquieu, another prominent philosophe, contributed ideas that challenged the structure of French government. His work *The Spirit of the Laws*, published in 1748, analyzed different forms of government and argued that **separation of**

powers was essential for a fair and just society. Montesquieu believed that political power should be divided among different branches of government—executive, legislative, and judicial—to prevent any one group or individual from becoming too powerful. This idea of checks and balances had a profound impact on political thought. While Montesquieu focused on England as a model, his ideas suggested a radical rethinking of France's absolute monarchy. In an Ancien Régime that concentrated power in the hands of the king, Montesquieu's ideas offered a vision of governance based on accountability and balance.

The concept of **natural rights** also gained traction during the Enlightenment, deeply influencing revolutionary thinkers. English philosopher **John Locke** was particularly instrumental in developing this idea, which argued that all people possess certain inherent rights simply by virtue of being human. Locke listed "life, liberty, and property" as fundamental rights that no government could justly infringe upon. Although Locke was English, his writings became widely read in France, where they inspired debates about personal freedom and individual rights. Locke's influence reached revolutionary leaders who saw the social order of the Ancien Régime as an unjust violation of these rights. The belief that individuals had inherent rights to freedom and security became a cornerstone of revolutionary thought, influencing the demands for a new legal and political order.

These Enlightenment ideas spread widely due to **salons and cafés**, which became centers of intellectual exchange. Salons were gatherings hosted by wealthy, often educated women in their homes, where writers, philosophers, and thinkers discussed politics, philosophy, and the latest ideas. Salons helped disseminate Enlightenment ideas among the elite and allowed for the exchange of radical views in a private setting. Cafés, on the other hand, were more accessible to the public and served as forums where the bourgeoisie, artisans, and even some commoners engaged in lively discussions about society and governance. The spread of pamphlets, books, and newspapers further facilitated the circulation of revolutionary ideas. Through these spaces, Enlightenment thought reached people of all backgrounds, fueling a growing discontent with the status quo.

Many in the **Third Estate**, particularly the bourgeoisie, embraced Enlightenment ideals as they looked at the privileges of the First and Second Estates. Educated members of this class read Rousseau, Voltaire, and Montesquieu and found in their writings a justification for challenging a system that denied them political rights and social recognition. The Enlightenment provided them with a language of **justice, equality, and rights**, concepts that they used to criticize the existing system. For many, these ideas offered a vision of a new society where merit and reason would replace inherited privilege.

The impact of the Enlightenment extended beyond intellectual circles and into the broader culture. Plays, essays, and satirical pieces criticized the monarchy and the Church, reaching an increasingly literate public. French dramatists and authors, inspired by the philosophes, used their works to expose the hypocrisy of the upper classes and the corruption of those in power. This cultural shift helped spread the belief that authority should not go unquestioned. People began to view the monarchy and the aristocracy not as natural rulers but as institutions that could—and should—be challenged. This shift in mindset laid the psychological groundwork for revolution, as people grew more willing to question long-standing traditions and structures.

The **Declaration of the Rights of Man and Citizen**, one of the most famous documents to emerge from the Revolution, directly reflected Enlightenment ideals. Written in 1789, it declared that "men are born and remain free and equal in rights." This statement echoed Rousseau's vision of equality and Locke's concept of natural rights. The Declaration outlined a society where law and governance would serve the people rather than ruling over them. It became a foundational document, not just for France but for democratic movements worldwide, encapsulating the Enlightenment's ideals of freedom, equality, and the rule of law.

The Enlightenment's emphasis on **rationality** and scientific progress also challenged religious authority. Although not all Enlightenment thinkers were atheists, many promoted a secular outlook, arguing that human reason, not divine will, should guide political and moral decisions. This secularism directly challenged the Catholic Church, which held significant power in France. The clergy's wealth, privileges, and influence over public life became increasingly suspect. As more people embraced a secular perspective, they saw the Church's control over education, moral guidance, and even political decisions as unjust and incompatible with a rational society.

In many ways, the Enlightenment was not a call for violence but a call for a society rooted in reason, rights, and equality. However, as these ideas spread, they exposed the **deep inequalities and injustices** within the Ancien Régime. People began to view the privileges of the aristocracy and clergy as obstacles to social progress. By challenging the existing power structures, the Enlightenment laid the ideological foundation for the French Revolution. Its thinkers did not set out to inspire a revolution, yet their ideas about human rights, governance, and equality resonated with a society that was increasingly aware of its own oppression. The Enlightenment did not cause the Revolution, but it provided the intellectual framework that made revolution thinkable.

Corruption and Inefficiency in Government

The French government in the years leading up to the Revolution was mired in **corruption and inefficiency**, affecting every level of administration. This dysfunction wasn't just a minor inconvenience; it deeply eroded public trust and exacerbated the social and economic problems that plagued the country. A web of bureaucracy, favoritism, and abuse of power led to government actions that were often slow, arbitrary, and disconnected from the needs of the French people. This system created bottlenecks for reforms, deepened class divides, and drove home the sense that France's rulers and officials were out of touch with reality.

At the top of the administration sat **Louis XVI**, whose indecisiveness worsened the government's inefficiency. Louis was neither a strong leader nor an effective manager of state affairs. Faced with France's mounting debt and social crises, he often hesitated to make decisions and avoided the bold reforms France so desperately needed. His inability to take decisive action left his ministers struggling to manage the government without clear guidance, resulting in a paralyzed administration that drifted from one crisis to the next. While Louis XVI was not inherently corrupt, his passivity allowed corruption to flourish among those who wielded power in his name.

The **nobility and clergy** held privileged positions within the government, often granted as rewards for loyalty rather than competence. Many high-ranking positions were not filled by those with skill or merit but by individuals born into aristocratic families or those who had purchased their offices. This system of **venality of office**, where positions were bought and sold, created a layer of officials whose primary interest was to recoup their investment rather than serve the public. This practice extended across the government, from judicial positions to tax collection and local administration. These officeholders, having paid for their positions, were more interested in leveraging their roles for personal gain than in fulfilling their duties honestly or effectively. As a result, local government officials often acted more like landlords, focusing on extracting wealth rather than helping communities thrive.

Tax collection was a notorious example of corruption in the Ancien Régime. Rather than collecting taxes directly, the crown outsourced this job to **tax farmers** —individuals or companies that paid the state for the right to collect taxes in specific regions. These tax farmers then collected taxes on behalf of the government, often charging peasants more than the official rate and pocketing the difference. It was a system ripe for abuse. The tax farmers would frequently engage in extortion, pushing peasants and townspeople to pay inflated rates to line their own pockets. The government, needing funds, turned a blind eye to these abuses, provided it received its share of revenue. This system not only burdened commoners with higher-than-necessary taxes but also created resentment toward both the tax farmers and the monarchy that supported them.

The **judicial system** was similarly corrupt and inefficient, offering little recourse for justice to the average citizen. Judges often purchased their positions, and many were members of the nobility who had little interest in the concerns of commoners. Cases moved slowly through the courts, especially for those who couldn't afford bribes or influence. The **parlements**, regional appellate courts, served as one of the few checks on royal power, but they operated with their own interests in mind, often obstructing reforms that threatened the privileges of the nobility. While these courts claimed to represent the people, they primarily acted to safeguard the aristocracy's interests. Consequently, for most citizens, the judicial system was inaccessible, biased, and costly, reinforcing the sense that the government was not there to serve them.

Another layer of government inefficiency came from the **intendant system**, designed to centralize control under the king but plagued by inflexibility. Intendants were royal officials appointed by the king to oversee provinces, ensuring they remained loyal to the crown. However, many intendants lacked knowledge of the regions they governed and acted with a heavy-handed approach that alienated local populations. Instead of understanding and responding to local needs, they enforced royal policies with little regard for their impacts on communities. The result was a disconnect between local governance and the centralized authority in Paris. Decisions made at the top often failed to consider the nuances of each region, leading to widespread dissatisfaction and further distrust of the monarchy.

Additionally, **administrative overlap** and poor coordination contributed to government inefficiency. France was divided into numerous provinces, each with its own customs, laws, and tax systems. Navigating these differences was a bureaucratic nightmare, as each province operated semi-autonomously. This lack of standardization meant that enforcing nationwide policies was challenging and inconsistent. The state had to contend with a maze of local laws and privileges, making any attempt at reform nearly impossible without resistance. Even minor changes required navigating through various local jurisdictions and often led to protracted battles with regional authorities. For citizens, this meant that government services were unreliable and inconsistent, varying widely depending on where one lived.

Meanwhile, the **military administration** suffered from a similar blend of corruption and inefficiency. Officers in the French army were primarily drawn from noble families, with commissions often bought rather than earned. As a result, the military was top-heavy with officers who had little training or experience in actual warfare. The common soldiers, mostly drawn from the lower classes, faced harsh conditions and received little pay or support. While France's military was one of the largest in Europe, its effectiveness was hampered by poor leadership and lack of investment in the rank-and-file. For those serving in the military, this unequal treatment reflected the broader social inequalities of the Ancien Régime, where the nobility enjoyed status and wealth while commoners bore the burdens.

Corruption also affected public spending and infrastructure development. Roads, bridges, and public works projects were often neglected or poorly executed, especially outside of Paris and major cities. When infrastructure projects were undertaken, funds often disappeared due to kickbacks and mismanagement, leaving communities with unfinished or poorly constructed roads and facilities. This neglect meant that rural areas remained isolated and economically disadvantaged, while urban centers struggled with inadequate infrastructure to support growing populations. The lack of investment in public services demonstrated the government's disregard for the well-being of the people, further alienating them from the state.

At the heart of this broken system was a deep **culture of patronage**. Favoritism and personal connections determined who held power and received royal attention, rather than competence or dedication to public service. The **royal court at**

Versailles was an extravagant center of this patronage system, where nobles and courtiers competed for the king's favor and vied for lucrative government positions. The court culture encouraged flattery, scheming, and intrigue, diverting attention from the nation's real issues. Ministers who dared to propose reforms found themselves outmaneuvered by powerful courtiers with vested interests in preserving the status quo. This court-centered governance distracted the monarchy from the pressing needs of the people, as resources and attention were devoted to maintaining the loyalty of nobles rather than addressing systemic problems.

The impact of these corrupt and inefficient systems went beyond mere inconvenience; they actively worsened the living conditions of most French citizens. Commoners paid heavy taxes yet saw few benefits. Local abuses, whether by tax farmers or judicial officials, created widespread resentment and reinforced the view that the government served only the elite. This sense of injustice fueled the spread of revolutionary ideas, as people began to see the existing system not just as ineffective but as fundamentally immoral and oppressive.

By the late 1780s, the weight of corruption and inefficiency had created a **governance crisis** that even the monarchy could not ignore. Financial mismanagement, abuse of office, and bureaucratic disorder left the state incapable of addressing mounting social and economic challenges. Efforts at reform, including proposals to simplify tax collection and reduce corruption, faced fierce resistance from those who benefitted from the system's flaws. The government's failure to correct these abuses deepened public frustration, eroding any remaining loyalty to the king and his administration.

When the Estates-General was called in 1789 to address the fiscal crisis, the Third Estate arrived with a long list of grievances, many related directly to government corruption and inefficiency. Representatives demanded not only fiscal reform but a complete restructuring of governance that would replace patronage and privilege with transparency and merit. The people wanted an accountable, fair system—a government that would respond to their needs rather than enrich a select few.

Influence of the American Revolution

The **American Revolution** had a profound impact on France, not only as a political event but as an inspiring model that exposed the French people to the idea that oppressive rule could be successfully challenged. The American struggle for independence began as a revolt against British colonial rule, but it quickly transformed into a powerful symbol of freedom, equality, and self-governance. France's involvement in this war, combined with the ideals that fueled the American Revolution, inspired new thinking among the French public and heightened existing frustrations with their own government.

French support for the American colonists was both political and strategic. The rivalry between France and Britain had a long history, and when the American colonies declared independence, France saw an opportunity to weaken its traditional enemy. By the 1770s, Britain was the dominant colonial power, and a British defeat in the Americas would shift the balance of power. **King Louis XVI** and his advisors saw a chance to restore French prestige after their losses in the Seven Years' War, which had ended with the humiliating Treaty of Paris in 1763. This treaty had forced France to cede much of its North American territory to Britain. Supporting the American Revolution offered a chance to strike back indirectly at the British and to regain some influence.

France committed substantial resources to the American cause, providing **money, troops, and naval support**. French officers, soldiers, and supplies were critical in key battles, and the French navy was instrumental in securing American victory, particularly in the decisive Battle of Yorktown. Figures like the Marquis de Lafayette, a young French nobleman who fought alongside the American forces, became heroes in France upon their return. Lafayette's experience in America profoundly influenced him; he returned to France as a passionate advocate for reform, carrying with him a vision of liberty and democracy inspired by his time in the United States.

The financial cost of the American Revolution was staggering. France had already been struggling with debt, but funding the war added significantly to this burden. Between 1775 and 1783, the French government poured millions of livres into the American effort. Loans taken out to finance the war effort added to France's already unsustainable debt levels, draining resources that might have been used to address internal needs. By the time the war ended, France was nearly bankrupt. The financial strain created by its support for the American Revolution only heightened the sense of economic crisis in France, leading to pressures that the monarchy could no longer ignore.

Beyond its economic impact, the American Revolution ignited **philosophical debates** among the French. The language of the **Declaration of Independence**, which stated that "all men are created equal" and endowed with "unalienable Rights" to "Life, Liberty, and the pursuit of Happiness," resonated deeply with French intellectuals and commoners alike. The Enlightenment ideals of equality, individual rights, and government by consent, already circulating in France, were given a new, practical example. The fact that these ideals were not just theoretical but had been used to create a new government in America gave them legitimacy and urgency. French people began to see that such principles could be realized, not just debated.

These ideas found eager audiences in **salons and cafés** across France, where intellectuals, writers, and reform-minded nobles gathered. Enlightenment philosophers like **Rousseau, Voltaire, and Montesquieu** had long argued for freedom, justice, and the idea of a social contract between rulers and the people. Now, the American Revolution seemed to confirm these philosophies, providing a concrete example of how they could be put into practice. French newspapers and pamphlets eagerly covered the progress of the American war, and accounts of the Revolution circulated widely. People across social classes absorbed the message that a government could be held accountable to its people.

The American Revolution also **emboldened the French bourgeoisie**—the wealthier, educated middle class that included merchants, lawyers, and intellectuals. The bourgeoisie already felt frustrated by their lack of political power, despite their economic influence. Seeing American colonists, many of whom were also wealthy merchants or landowners, take up arms for representation and rights was a powerful motivator. Many in the French bourgeoisie saw themselves as parallel to the American revolutionaries: economically significant but politically powerless under an outdated monarchy. They wanted a government that reflected their interests and respected their role in society.

Furthermore, **French soldiers** who fought in the American Revolution returned home with new ideas and experiences. They had witnessed a people willing to fight for their freedom and establish a government based on democratic principles. These soldiers, many from lower ranks, had shared in the American victory and felt its significance deeply. They returned to France carrying the spirit of rebellion and independence, which only deepened the dissatisfaction with their own conditions. The ideas of individual rights and representative government had become more than abstract ideals; they were principles that these soldiers had seen in action, adding weight to their demands for change.

In addition to soldiers, other influential figures, such as **Benjamin Franklin and Thomas Jefferson**, visited France during and after the Revolution, furthering French enthusiasm for the American cause. Franklin, who arrived in France in 1776 as an ambassador, was especially popular. His diplomatic charm, wit, and plain manner won over many French nobles and intellectuals, and he became a celebrated figure in Parisian society. Franklin's presence brought American values directly to France's social and political elite, where he mingled with leading figures in the French Enlightenment. Thomas Jefferson, who became the American ambassador to France in 1785, also formed close connections with influential French thinkers and politicians, promoting the values that had shaped the new American republic.

For ordinary French citizens, the American Revolution was a beacon of hope. Many French commoners faced high taxes, poor harvests, and limited opportunities under a system that offered them few rights or protections. The success of the American Revolution suggested that these hardships were not inevitable. If a distant group of colonists could fight for their freedom and create a new society, why couldn't the French people demand similar rights? This question began to weigh on the minds of peasants, urban workers, and artisans, who saw the American Revolution as proof that ordinary people could challenge the injustices of the powerful.

The influence of the American Revolution also extended to **political reformers within France** who saw it as a chance to argue for concrete changes. Some reformers proposed limiting the power of the monarchy or establishing a representative assembly that would give voice to all estates. They pointed to

America's success as evidence that a society based on equal representation and accountability could work. Reform-minded nobles and clergy, who had read the works of Rousseau and Montesquieu, began to question whether the French monarchy truly served the best interests of the people. The American experiment in self-governance inspired them to consider alternatives to absolute monarchy.

The events in America also **exposed contradictions in French governance**. While supporting the American colonies' fight for liberty, the French government itself continued to deny rights to its own people. The hypocrisy was striking: a French monarchy fighting for freedom abroad while enforcing strict control at home. This disconnect between France's foreign policy and domestic reality fueled discontent. French citizens increasingly viewed the monarchy as an obstacle to justice and liberty, and they questioned why their rulers would support freedom in another country while maintaining such a rigid structure at home.

All of these influences—the economic strain, the inspiration of revolutionary ideas, the influence on French soldiers, and the contradiction of French foreign policy—added to the **growing discontent** within France. The American Revolution showed the French that transformation was possible, and it provided a clear blueprint for achieving it. As the financial crisis worsened, demands for change grew louder, and the ideals that had once seemed abstract became demands for tangible reform.

The French people, inspired by what they saw in America, began to imagine a new France, one where government would protect their rights and where power would no longer rest solely in the hands of a privileged few. The American Revolution had proven that such dreams were not merely fantasies but attainable goals. With the stage set by these ideals and by the increasingly unbearable strains on society, the seeds of revolution in France began to take root.

Early Revolutionary Sentiments and Movements

Early revolutionary sentiments in France didn't begin with large crowds storming palaces or tearing down institutions; they started in discussions, writings, and small gatherings. By the late 1780s, frustration with the monarchy and the privileged classes had spread across much of French society. A shared sense of injustice began to build among diverse groups, each with their own grievances, yet all unified in the belief that change was both possible and necessary. **Intellectuals, workers, and even some members of the nobility started questioning the system**, laying the groundwork for the revolutionary movements that would soon take shape.

Among the **bourgeoisie**, the wealthier and educated members of the Third Estate, ideas of reform were especially strong. The bourgeoisie included merchants, professionals, and intellectuals—people who were economically significant but politically powerless. This class resented the privileges of the nobility and the exclusion from positions of influence, despite their wealth and knowledge. They had long read the works of Enlightenment thinkers like Rousseau, Montesquieu, and Voltaire, who promoted ideas of equality, individual rights, and government accountability. Enlightenment ideals offered the bourgeoisie a language to critique the monarchy, advocating for a society based on reason, equality, and justice rather than birthright and privilege. They wanted to end the arbitrary distinctions that kept them locked out of political power, and they began to form small groups where they discussed the possibility of a new social order.

The **café culture** in Paris became a breeding ground for these early revolutionary ideas. Cafés served as public spaces where people from different backgrounds could gather, discuss, and share news. They became unofficial forums where political issues and grievances were debated openly, and the ideas of the Enlightenment circulated widely. Here, discussions that might have once seemed dangerous grew common. People spoke openly about the abuses of the monarchy, the greed of the nobility, and the failure of the government to address the needs of the people. The cafés provided a unique setting where both the bourgeoisie and the working class could mingle, creating an environment in which revolutionary sentiments could cross social boundaries.

In addition to cafés, **salons** held by influential women such as Madame Roland and Madame de Staël brought together intellectuals, writers, and reform-minded nobles. These salons were gatherings that allowed participants to debate ideas, share writings, and critique society without the restrictions imposed by formal institutions. Salon hosts often encouraged discussions on topics ranging from political reform to individual rights, and they were influential in spreading revolutionary ideas among the upper classes. For many nobles, participation in these salons exposed them to the grievances of the Third Estate and offered a new perspective on the inequalities built into French society.

Another key force in stirring early revolutionary sentiments was the **press**. By the late 1780s, France had a growing print culture, with newspapers, pamphlets, and books reaching a larger audience than ever before. Writers like **Jean-Paul Marat** and **Camille Desmoulins** used the press to expose government corruption, criticize the monarchy, and demand change. Marat, a passionate and often inflammatory writer, published *L'Ami du peuple* (The Friend of the People), a newspaper that became immensely popular among ordinary citizens. His writings condemned the aristocracy and called for justice, often using fiery language that resonated with those who felt ignored by the ruling class. Desmoulins, on the other hand, was known for his wit and persuasive arguments. His pamphlets and speeches inspired many to support revolutionary ideas, framing the need for reform in terms that the average citizen could understand.

One pivotal moment that crystallized these revolutionary sentiments came in **1787**, when **Louis XVI** called the Assembly of Notables to discuss financial reform. The country's debt was spiraling, and the king needed approval to impose new taxes, especially on the nobility, who had long been exempt. This assembly included nobles and clergy, who were unwilling to give up their privileges or support the proposed reforms. The failure of the Assembly of Notables highlighted the government's inability to reform itself and reinforced the view that the privileged classes would never sacrifice their own interests for the common good. This failure set the stage for broader calls to convene the **Estates-General**, a representative assembly that had not been called since 1614. Many saw this as an opportunity for the people to voice their grievances, and the call to gather the Estates-General fueled hopes for meaningful change.

The **Third Estate** quickly began organizing in anticipation of the Estates-General, which was finally scheduled for May 1789. Across the country, representatives from the Third Estate gathered to compile lists of grievances, known as **cahiers de doléances**. These lists cataloged the issues faced by common people, ranging from high taxes and feudal dues to demands for freedom of speech and equal representation. The cahiers provided a rare opportunity for ordinary citizens to communicate their frustrations to the government directly, and the process itself raised awareness and mobilized people to participate in the political process. As these grievances were collected, a sense of unity began to emerge within the Third Estate, as people recognized shared struggles and collective goals.

When the Estates-General finally convened, tensions quickly surfaced over **voting procedures**. Traditionally, each estate cast one vote as a bloc, meaning that the clergy and nobility could outvote the Third Estate two to one, despite representing a small fraction of the population. The Third Estate demanded that voting be based on headcount rather than estate, giving them fairer representation. When the king refused this request, the representatives of the Third Estate took a bold step. On June 17, 1789, they declared themselves the **National Assembly**, asserting that they represented the will of the French people. This was a direct challenge to the king's authority and marked the beginning of a new political reality.

The decision to form the National Assembly was a defining moment, and it soon led to the famous **Tennis Court Oath** on June 20, 1789. After being locked out of their usual meeting hall, the members of the Third Estate gathered in a nearby indoor tennis court and vowed not to disband until they had created a constitution for France. This oath represented a powerful act of defiance, symbolizing the determination of the Third Estate to push forward with their demands for a fairer society. The Tennis Court Oath unified the Third Estate and gave a clear purpose to the movement, solidifying their commitment to bringing change, regardless of the king's resistance.

These early actions by the National Assembly sparked **widespread support among commoners**. In Paris and other major cities, people began to openly resist the monarchy and support the Assembly's decisions. Pamphlets, speeches, and public gatherings spread news of the Tennis Court Oath and the formation of the National Assembly, rallying people behind the cause. On the streets, rumors circulated about potential crackdowns by the monarchy, leading to heightened tensions. The common people, already suffering from food shortages and high taxes, saw in the Assembly a voice that echoed their own frustrations.

The early revolutionary movement took on an increasingly **radical tone** with the **storming of the Bastille** on July 14, 1789. The Bastille, a fortress and prison in Paris, symbolized the monarchy's absolute power. When angry crowds stormed the Bastille, it was not merely a rebellion against a building; it was an attack on a symbol of oppression. The fall of the Bastille was a signal to both the king and the people that the old system was vulnerable. The people's successful takeover of the fortress emboldened revolutionary sentiments, proving that popular action could challenge and even overcome royal authority.

In the countryside, the early revolutionary sentiment manifested in what became known as the **Great Fear**. Peasants, long oppressed by feudal obligations, heard rumors that nobles were plotting to suppress the revolution with violent force. In response, many peasants took matters into their own hands, attacking manor houses, burning records of feudal dues, and seizing land. This uprising in rural areas showed that revolutionary fervor was not confined to the cities; it had spread to the farthest reaches of France, where peasants saw the revolution as a chance to rid themselves of centuries-old burdens.

As these early revolutionary actions unfolded, they were not isolated events but a **growing wave of resistance**. People from various backgrounds and regions came together, each driven by different reasons but united by a shared discontent. The sense that change was possible electrified the population, pushing them to take bolder steps and to envision a society free from the constraints of the Ancien Régime. What had begun as sentiments of frustration and discussions in cafés and salons had quickly grown into a powerful movement that would soon reshape France entirely. The early revolutionary sentiments had taken hold, and there was no turning back.

CHAPTER 2: THE MEETING OF THE ESTATES-GENERAL

The Calling of the Estates-General

The **calling of the Estates-General** in 1789 was an event that France had not seen in nearly 175 years. Since 1614, this assembly—a body that included representatives from the three estates: the clergy, the nobility, and the commoners—had been absent from French politics. By the late 1780s, however, France's financial crisis had reached a point of no return. Years of debt from wars, overspending by the monarchy, and an unequal tax system had drained the nation's resources. King Louis XVI found himself with few options and intense pressure from nearly every segment of society. Out of desperation, he made the historic decision to call the Estates-General, hoping it could provide solutions to the financial crisis and restore stability.

The Estates-General was traditionally an **advisory body**, not a legislative one. Although its representatives had gathered periodically throughout the medieval and early modern periods, they had no real power to enact laws. Instead, the assembly served as a means for the king to consult the different social classes and, in times of crisis, seek their support. In practice, however, the king could choose to ignore their advice. But this time, Louis XVI had far fewer options. The French treasury was empty, and the people, especially those in the Third Estate, were burdened by heavy taxes while the nobility and clergy enjoyed exemptions. Without the Estates-General's support for new taxes, Louis was trapped between the nobles' resistance and the commoners' demands for reform.

The process of calling the Estates-General began in 1788 when Louis XVI issued an **edict** to convene the assembly. This decision was met with mixed reactions. For many in the nobility, the Estates-General represented an opportunity to secure their privileges and possibly avoid new taxes. Nobles hoped to use the assembly to assert their influence over the king and resist changes that threatened their traditional exemptions. Meanwhile, the Third Estate saw it as a rare chance to address their grievances directly and push for reforms that would alleviate their suffering and grant them a voice in government. While the upper estates viewed the assembly as a way to preserve their advantages, the Third Estate had far more ambitious goals for change.

The assembly was to include representatives from all three estates. Each estate would elect its representatives separately, with the clergy and nobility selecting members from among their ranks, while the Third Estate held elections across France to choose its delegates. **In total, the Estates-General would consist of over 1,200 representatives**: around 300 clergy members, 300 nobles, and roughly 600 representatives from the Third Estate. The king agreed to double the number of representatives for the Third Estate, a move intended to give the commoners more representation. However, this concession did little to address a fundamental issue: the method of voting. Traditionally, each estate voted as a bloc, casting one collective vote, rather than individual votes for each representative. This meant that the First and Second Estates could easily outvote the Third Estate, despite representing a much smaller portion of the population.

The question of voting became a central issue long before the Estates-General convened. **The Third Estate demanded voting by headcount**, where each representative's vote would count individually, rather than by estate. This change would allow the Third Estate to leverage its larger numbers and push through reforms that had long been blocked by the nobility and clergy. However, both the king and the privileged estates resisted this demand, fearing that headcount voting would shift the balance of power toward the commoners. For the Third Estate, voting by headcount was not simply a technical detail; it represented a step toward political equality and a way to challenge the rigid class divisions that had governed France for centuries.

Before the Estates-General met, the government requested that each estate compile **cahiers de doléances**, or "notebooks of grievances." These documents allowed communities across France to list their complaints, concerns, and demands, providing a snapshot of the nation's discontent. Peasants expressed anger over feudal dues and taxes that kept them in poverty. The bourgeoisie demanded political representation and the abolition of privileges that unfairly protected the nobility and clergy. Even some clergy members, especially those from poorer parishes, voiced support for reforms that would benefit the lower classes. These grievance lists exposed the depth of dissatisfaction within France and highlighted the wide range of issues that the Estates-General would need to address. From rural villages to bustling cities, the voices of the people echoed with demands for change.

As the representatives of the estates traveled to Versailles, the atmosphere was tense. The French people held high hopes that the Estates-General would finally address their hardships. For many, this assembly symbolized the possibility of a new order—an opportunity to confront injustice and reshape society. In Paris and other urban centers, citizens gathered to discuss their expectations, and public interest soared. The press covered every development, and pamphlets circulated, analyzing what the assembly might achieve. People were keenly aware that the Estates-General represented more than just a response to a financial crisis; it was a chance to rewrite the social contract.

When the Estates-General opened on **May 5, 1789**, the king's speech focused on the economic crisis and the need for financial reforms. However, he avoided addressing the broader grievances outlined in the cahiers. Louis XVI's reluctance to discuss structural reforms disappointed the representatives, particularly those from the Third Estate, who had hoped for more substantial changes. The king's insistence on focusing solely on finances revealed his reluctance to challenge the privileged estates and tackle the root causes of France's problems. His lack of vision and determination left the assembly with no clear path forward, setting the stage for escalating conflict.

The **deadlock over voting procedures** quickly brought tensions to a boiling point. For weeks, the representatives debated and argued, but the king refused to endorse voting by headcount, and the First and Second Estates resisted any shift in power. The Third Estate, feeling increasingly marginalized, grew frustrated. They had come to Versailles with the hope of fair representation and reform, yet found themselves outmaneuvered by the entrenched interests of the nobility and clergy. For the commoners, the Estates-General seemed to be descending into a repeat of past assemblies, where the voices of the many were silenced by the privileges of the few.

The standoff reached a critical moment when the Third Estate decided to **act independently**. On June 17, 1789, they boldly declared themselves the **National Assembly**, claiming that they alone represented the people of France. This declaration was a direct challenge to the existing order, asserting that sovereignty belonged not to the king or the aristocracy but to the nation itself. The formation of the National Assembly marked a pivotal moment in the Revolution, symbolizing the commoners' refusal to be excluded from political power. They were no longer asking for reform; they were taking control.

The king's response was hesitant and contradictory. At first, he attempted to ignore the declaration, hoping that the Third Estate's boldness would fade. However, the representatives of the National Assembly continued to meet, gathering support from some sympathetic clergy and even a few nobles. Seeing that the National Assembly would not back down, Louis XVI eventually ordered the closure of their meeting hall, hoping to disrupt their activities. Undeterred, the Assembly moved to an indoor tennis court, where they took the famous **Tennis Court Oath**, vowing not to disband until they had created a constitution for France. This oath became a defining act of defiance, representing the determination of the Third Estate to push forward, regardless of royal resistance.

The calling of the Estates-General had set the Revolution in motion. What began as an attempt to address a financial crisis had evolved into a fundamental conflict over representation, rights, and the distribution of power. By refusing to yield on the issue of voting by headcount, the monarchy and the privileged estates had unwittingly united the Third Estate against them. The representatives of the Third Estate, now the National Assembly, had taken their first steps toward dismantling the Ancien Régime, igniting a revolutionary movement that would reshape France forever.

Tensions Between the Estates

From the moment the Estates-General gathered in 1789, tensions between the three estates—clergy, nobility, and commoners—were unmistakable. The Third

Estate, representing nearly 98% of the French population, arrived in Versailles burdened by high hopes but low expectations of fair treatment. They came with extensive lists of grievances that called for relief from crushing taxes, the end of feudal dues, and equal representation. Yet, as the Estates-General convened, it became clear that neither the First Estate (the clergy) nor the Second Estate (the nobility) had any intention of ceding their privileges or adopting the reforms demanded by the commoners.

Each estate's representatives viewed the assembly differently. The **clergy**, which represented about 0.5% of the population, was internally divided. Parish priests, or *curés*, often came from humble backgrounds and sympathized with the Third Estate's calls for reform. However, the higher-ranking clergy, often drawn from noble families, saw any reform as a threat to their wealth, influence, and the Church's control over French society. These upper clergy members were highly resistant to changes that could diminish their social and economic privileges. The divide between parish priests and high-ranking bishops highlighted growing splits within the First Estate itself, reflecting larger societal fractures.

Meanwhile, the **Second Estate**, comprising the nobility, felt their privileges slipping away and were determined to hold on. Nobles saw themselves as guardians of French tradition and believed their status entitled them to special rights, including exemption from most taxes. Many of them had gained their wealth and power through centuries of inherited titles and land ownership, and they feared that reform would strip them of these advantages. The nobility's sense of entitlement ran deep, and their disdain for the Third Estate's demands was palpable. Although some progressive nobles sympathized with Enlightenment ideas and recognized the need for reform, the majority viewed any change as a direct assault on the social order that had secured their privileged positions.

The **Third Estate** found itself united against the aristocracy and the clergy, but within its ranks, there were also divisions. The bourgeoisie—educated, wealthy members of the middle class, including merchants, lawyers, and professionals—had different concerns from the peasantry and urban workers. While the bourgeoisie pushed for representation and tax reform, peasants were more concerned with ending feudal dues and reducing the Church's influence over daily life. However, despite these internal differences, the representatives of the Third Estate were bound together by a shared sense of exclusion and frustration. They were painfully aware that the traditional voting structure, where each estate cast a single vote as a bloc, would inevitably work against them, allowing the clergy and nobility to outvote them at every turn.

The **debate over voting procedures** quickly became a flashpoint for conflict. The Third Estate demanded voting by headcount rather than by estate, arguing that this would more accurately reflect the will of the people, given that they represented the overwhelming majority of the population. The clergy and nobility, however, rejected this demand, as it would shift power toward the commoners. For them, headcount voting was an unacceptable challenge to their authority, as it would place decision-making power into the hands of those they considered socially and economically inferior. This deadlock over voting intensified feelings of alienation among the Third Estate, who saw it as proof that the privileged classes would never willingly share power.

In response, the **Third Estate grew increasingly defiant**. As days passed, they became more outspoken, making public speeches and circulating pamphlets that condemned the inequality of the Estates-General. The press reported these events widely, and news spread rapidly, reaching the streets of Paris and other French cities. Many representatives of the Third Estate began to speak openly about their dissatisfaction with the monarchy and the failure of the Estates-General to address the true needs of the people. Anger simmered in the assembly halls as commoners looked across the room at the well-dressed clergy and nobility, who seemed indifferent to their suffering and sacrifices.

Some members of the clergy, particularly the parish priests, grew sympathetic to the Third Estate's demands. They saw firsthand the poverty and hardship of the common people and felt that the Church had an obligation to support just reform. However, these voices were often drowned out by the powerful bishops and high-ranking clergy who dominated the First Estate. The divide within the clergy created further complications, as some priests began meeting privately with representatives of the Third Estate, forging alliances that were highly unusual in a society so strictly divided by class.

The nobility, feeling under siege, responded with hostility. Many noble representatives viewed the Third Estate's demands as a betrayal of the traditional values that held French society together. They saw the commoners as unruly upstarts, and their resistance to voting reforms and other demands became more entrenched as they feared that any concession might lead to a loss of their own status and privileges. By refusing to compromise, they deepened the divide between themselves and the Third Estate, fueling the resentment and frustration that would soon explode into open rebellion.

The **standoff grew more intense** each day, and with every refusal by the privileged estates to address their demands, the Third Estate grew more convinced that radical action was needed. They realized that the structure of the Estates-General was designed to keep power in the hands of the few and prevent any real change. The representatives of the Third Estate, sensing that they had little to lose, began to strategize ways to assert their own power. Tensions were high, and it was clear that the Estates-General could not proceed as the king and nobility had hoped.

The Rise of the Third Estate

The Third Estate entered the Estates-General with the least power but the highest expectations. Their numbers and grievances far outweighed those of the clergy and nobility, and they were determined to have a say in shaping the future of France. Representatives from the Third Estate came from all over the country and represented every level of society, from wealthy merchants and educated lawyers to small farmers and artisans. Despite their differences, they shared a common frustration: they bore the tax burden, suffered under feudal dues, and had little to no political power. As they gathered in Versailles, their shared hardships created a sense of unity and purpose, setting the stage for a bold assertion of their rights.

Initially, the Third Estate demanded **voting by headcount** in the Estates-General, a change that would allow each representative to vote individually, giving them a fairer share of power. The king and the privileged estates, however, refused this demand, insisting on the traditional one-vote-per-estate system. This rejection intensified the Third Estate's resolve. They realized that if they were to achieve meaningful change, they could not depend on the goodwill of the nobility or clergy. Instead, they would need to act independently to assert their influence and achieve the representation they believed was their due.

The decision to form the **National Assembly** on June 17, 1789, marked the rise of the Third Estate as a powerful political force. With this declaration, they asserted that they represented the people of France and claimed the authority to act on the nation's behalf. This bold step signaled a shift from a passive to an active role in French politics. The representatives no longer saw themselves merely as petitioners; they saw themselves as a sovereign body capable of deciding France's future. This self-proclaimed authority was a direct challenge to the king's power, symbolizing a fundamental break from the old order.

The act of forming the National Assembly ignited a **wave of support** from across France. Commoners, who had long felt ignored and exploited, saw in the Third Estate a group willing to stand up for their interests. For the first time, they felt that their voices were being represented in the halls of power. News of the National Assembly spread quickly, and people from cities to rural villages began to rally behind the commoners at Versailles. The streets of Paris buzzed with excitement and hope as citizens gathered to discuss these developments, seeing in the Third Estate's actions the potential for a new France.

This newfound confidence led to the **Tennis Court Oath** on June 20, 1789, a pivotal event that underscored the Third Estate's determination. After being locked out of their meeting hall, the representatives of the National Assembly gathered in a nearby indoor tennis court. There, they vowed not to disband until they had drafted a new constitution for France. This oath was more than a simple promise; it was a declaration of purpose. The Third Estate was no longer merely demanding reforms—they were asserting their right to create a new foundation for French society. It was an act of defiance and unity that solidified the Third Estate's rise as a revolutionary force.

As the Third Estate continued to grow in strength and resolve, even some members of the First Estate, primarily lower-ranking clergy, began to defect and join the National Assembly in a remarkable act of solidarity. These clerical defectors, often from humble backgrounds and familiar with the daily struggles of ordinary citizens, recognized the legitimacy of the commoners' demands for fair representation and relief from oppressive taxation. They understood that the future of France lay with the will of the people rather than the privileges of a wealthy few. By crossing over to join the National Assembly, these members of the clergy not only validated the grievances of the Third Estate but also symbolized a break in the previously unyielding hierarchical structures that defined the Ancien Régime.

Their defection was a powerful signal that the calls for change were reaching beyond the commoners to those within the privileged estates. This alliance between the Third Estate and sympathetic members of the clergy transformed what had been a struggle for political representation into a broader movement for social justice and reform.

CHAPTER 3: THE TENNIS COURT OATH AND FORMATION OF THE NATIONAL ASSEMBLY

The Significance of the Tennis Court Oath

The **Tennis Court Oath** was a defining moment in the early days of the French Revolution, an act of defiance that captured the determination and unity of the Third Estate in their pursuit of political change. On June 20, 1789, after being locked out of their usual meeting place at Versailles, representatives of the Third Estate gathered in a nearby indoor tennis court. Here, they took an oath not to disband until they had written a new constitution for France. This simple act carried enormous significance, symbolizing the collective will of the people to demand change and challenging the authority of the monarchy in an unprecedented way.

The symbolic power of the Tennis Court Oath lay in its **bold claim to sovereignty**. By declaring themselves the National Assembly and refusing to adjourn until a constitution was created, the representatives of the Third Estate took the first decisive step away from the king's authority. Up to that point, the monarchy and the privileged estates—the clergy and the nobility—had held near-total control over French society. But the Tennis Court Oath rejected this structure. Instead of accepting the king's authority as absolute, the assembly asserted that power lay with the people and that the representatives gathered there were accountable to the nation, not the king. This was a powerful statement that went far beyond the immediate circumstances, striking at the heart of the Ancien Régime's system of inherited privilege.

The oath **unified the Third Estate** in a way that other events had not. The representatives who swore the oath came from all walks of life, from prosperous bourgeoisie to farmers, each bringing with them the concerns and frustrations of their communities. France's deep social divisions had long made unity difficult, even among the Third Estate. Yet in that tennis court, these differences seemed to melt away. The representatives shared a sense of purpose, bound together by a common goal and a collective struggle against a system that had oppressed them. By pledging not to disband until they had achieved their goal, they created a sense of camaraderie that would be crucial in the Revolution's next stages. They were no longer individuals representing isolated grievances; they were now a single, united body with a clear mission.

The Third Estate's determination in the Tennis Court Oath **emboldened others across France**. News of the event spread quickly, and common people, especially in Paris, felt inspired by the representatives' courage. The oath gave ordinary citizens a rallying point, something to believe in. It showed that the people's voice could stand up to centuries-old systems of privilege and power. In towns and villages, people began to gather and express their support for the National Assembly. They saw in the Tennis Court Oath a vision of a new France, one where the people could take control of their own destinies. The assembly's act was not just about demanding rights; it was about laying the foundation for a nation built on those rights.

The **king's reaction to the oath** only underscored its significance. Louis XVI tried to ignore the assembly at first, dismissing their demands as temporary outrage. But as the assembly continued to meet and attract attention, he realized that this was more than just a protest. Yet he hesitated, uncertain how to handle this defiance without sparking further unrest. By hesitating, he revealed the monarchy's weakness and reluctance to confront the assembly head-on. For the people watching, the king's response showed that the power of the monarchy was not as absolute as it appeared. The Tennis Court Oath exposed the monarchy's vulnerability, planting the idea that the old order was not as unshakable as it seemed.

The oath was also significant for its **impact on members of the other estates**. Some parish priests from the First Estate and a few nobles from the Second Estate began to side with the Third Estate after the oath. For the clergy, especially those who came from humble backgrounds, the assembly's demand for reform aligned with their own experiences of witnessing poverty and suffering among their congregations. Some members of the nobility who had sympathies with Enlightenment ideas saw the Tennis Court Oath as a bold affirmation of those values. Their support helped validate the assembly's actions and showed that the push for change was not limited to a single class. The assembly, now backed by members across estates, had transformed the movement into a broader coalition with the potential to reshape French society.

The **Tennis Court Oath also marked a turning point** in the assembly's relationship with the king. No longer content to wait for royal permission, the National Assembly claimed authority independently. This was a direct challenge to the idea of divine right, which had justified the monarchy's rule for centuries. The Third Estate's insistence on drafting a constitution without the king's approval was a revolutionary idea in itself. It questioned the very foundation of monarchy, suggesting that power came from the people, not from a ruler chosen by God. For a society steeped in the tradition of absolute monarchy, this was a radical notion, one that would pave the way for further challenges to the king's authority.

In a practical sense, the oath **set the stage for the drafting of a constitution** that would define the future of France. By vowing to create a new framework for government, the National Assembly made it clear that they sought to go beyond superficial reforms. They wanted to build a political system rooted in the principles of justice, equality, and representation. This commitment to creating a constitution reflected the influence of Enlightenment ideas, especially those of Rousseau, Montesquieu, and Locke, who had argued for government as a social contract based on the consent of the governed. The Tennis Court Oath represented the moment when these ideas were no longer abstract philosophies but guiding principles for real political action.

Finally, the **Tennis Court Oath had a psychological impact on France**. It gave people a new way to think about power and authority. The idea that common representatives, meeting in a plain indoor court rather than a palace or cathedral, could lay the foundation for a new nation resonated across France. It broke down the old image of authority as something grand and distant, showing instead that power could come from humble places and from ordinary people. This realization sparked a new sense of empowerment among the French, a belief that they too could influence their country's future. The oath symbolized a transfer of authority from the king to the people, creating a precedent for future revolutionary actions.

Creation of the National Assembly

The **creation of the National Assembly** was a defining moment in the French Revolution, one that marked the beginning of a fundamental shift in power from the monarchy to the people. Frustrated by the rigid and unfair system of the Estates-General, which had been called to address France's financial crisis, the Third Estate took bold steps to assert its authority. The Estates-General, summoned by King Louis XVI in 1789, brought representatives from the First Estate (the clergy), the Second Estate (the nobility), and the Third Estate (the commoners) to Versailles. However, the voting structure was deeply unequal. Each estate voted as a single bloc, meaning the privileged clergy and nobility, who made up only a small fraction of France's population, could easily overrule the much larger Third Estate. This arrangement made any meaningful reform nearly impossible.

As discussions unfolded, members of the Third Estate quickly grew frustrated with their lack of influence. They represented over 95% of the population, yet they had the same voting power as each of the much smaller First and Second Estates. The Third Estate demanded **double representation** to reflect its population size, and while the king initially granted this, he refused to alter the voting system. Each estate would still vote as a bloc, effectively nullifying the Third Estate's larger numbers. This refusal signaled to the representatives of the Third Estate that the monarchy and the upper estates had little interest in addressing their grievances or giving them a genuine voice.

Determined to act, the Third Estate declared themselves the **National Assembly** on June 17, 1789. This bold declaration was a step toward asserting their authority, claiming that they represented the will of the French people. The National Assembly aimed to enact reforms and draft a new constitution that would limit the monarchy's powers and guarantee rights for the common people. By declaring themselves a new legislative body, they broke away from the traditional structure of the Estates-General, which had upheld France's feudal and aristocratic system. This move was revolutionary in itself, as it was a clear assertion that sovereignty belonged to the people rather than the king or the privileged few.

King Louis XVI's reaction to the creation of the National Assembly was one of alarm and resistance. He quickly ordered the hall where the National Assembly was meeting to be closed, hoping to disrupt their plans. Undeterred, the members of the National Assembly relocated to a nearby indoor tennis court, where they took what would become known as the **Tennis Court Oath**. In this oath, they vowed not to disband until they had written a new constitution for France. This act of defiance was a turning point, both symbolically and practically, as it underscored the Assembly's determination to establish a new political order. Their oath demonstrated a unity and resolve that would inspire revolutionary fervor across France.

The **National Assembly's creation** reflected a shift in revolutionary sentiment from mere reform to a complete rethinking of France's political system. In previous calls for reform, the Third Estate had largely sought to address specific grievances, such as high taxes and exclusion from decision-making. However, in forming the National Assembly, they were making a broader claim for sovereignty. They rejected the authority of the king to determine their role, and they assumed the authority to act on behalf of the entire French nation. This move challenged the idea that political power came from the monarchy or the nobility; instead, it insisted that legitimate power could only come from the people.

As word spread of the Assembly's defiance, **support grew from within and outside the Assembly**. Some members of the First Estate, particularly those from lower ranks of the clergy who had close ties with commoners, crossed over and joined the Assembly, signaling that even parts of the privileged estates recognized the need for change. These defections added legitimacy to the Assembly's claims and weakened the monarchy's position. In contrast, most members of the Second Estate, the nobility, remained aligned with the monarchy, viewing the Assembly's actions as a direct threat to their privileges and status.

The National Assembly's efforts did not go unchallenged. The king and his advisors initially saw this new body as illegal, fearing that it undermined royal authority and stability. King Louis XVI vacillated, torn between calls for military intervention to suppress the Assembly and advice to accept some degree of reform. Ultimately, he attempted a strategy of appeasement, recognizing the National Assembly but simultaneously ordering troops to gather around Paris and Versailles. This show of force heightened tensions and made many believe that the king was preparing to dissolve the Assembly by force.

This **standoff between the National Assembly and the monarchy** set the stage for greater upheaval. The presence of troops in Paris fueled popular unrest, as rumors spread that the king planned to use force to suppress the Assembly and its supporters. The people of Paris, already suffering from food shortages and economic hardship, rallied in support of the Assembly. On July 14, this tension erupted into the **Storming of the Bastille**, a fortress and prison that symbolized royal tyranny. The fall of the Bastille was a powerful signal of the people's power, and it marked a point of no return. With the Bastille's fall, the king's authority was openly challenged, and the National Assembly solidified its position as the legitimate government.

The National Assembly quickly moved to address the people's grievances and dismantle the structures of the Ancien Régime. In August 1789, the Assembly passed the **August Decrees**, which abolished feudal privileges and effectively ended the feudal system in France. These decrees meant that peasants were no longer subject to dues or obligations to their local lords, and the nobility lost many of their hereditary rights and privileges. The National Assembly also issued the **Declaration of the Rights of Man and of the Citizen**, a groundbreaking document that enshrined principles of equality, liberty, and popular sovereignty. This declaration became a cornerstone of the Revolution, asserting that all men were born free and equal and that government should protect citizens' natural rights.

As the National Assembly continued its work, it faced the enormous challenge of **drafting a constitution** that balanced revolutionary ideals with practical governance. The process was fraught with debate, as factions within the Assembly disagreed over the structure of the new government, the extent of royal power, and the role of the Church. Some favored a constitutional monarchy, while others advocated for a republic. The question of whether to limit or abolish the monarchy created rifts that would define the Revolution's course, as debates over the role of the king intensified.

The National Assembly's actions sparked similar movements across France. Local communities formed their own assemblies, challenging traditional authorities and demanding greater political voice. Revolutionary clubs, such as the **Jacobins** and the **Cordeliers**, emerged to discuss and promote revolutionary ideas. These clubs were influential in mobilizing public opinion and pushing the Revolution toward more radical goals. Inspired by the National Assembly's stance, citizens began to see themselves not as subjects under royal rule but as active participants in shaping their government and society.

As the National Assembly's influence grew, so did the challenges it faced. **Opposition from the king, the nobility, and conservative factions** continued to threaten the Revolution's progress. Meanwhile, tensions between France and other European powers were escalating, as monarchs across Europe watched with alarm. Many feared that revolutionary ideas would spread beyond France's borders, threatening their own rule. The threat of foreign intervention became a pressing concern, influencing the Assembly's decisions and pushing the Revolution into new phases as it sought to defend itself.

The creation of the National Assembly represented a **radical reimagining of political power in France**, one in which sovereignty belonged to the people rather than to a king or nobility. By establishing itself as the voice of the nation, the National Assembly ignited a process of reform that would transform not only the government but also the fabric of French society. This shift in power laid the groundwork for the Revolution's later stages, setting in motion events that would lead to the downfall of the monarchy and the establishment of a republic. In forming the National Assembly, the Third Estate had effectively asserted the people's right to self-governance, a right that would become a central tenet of modern democratic principles.

The Declaration of Intent for Change

The National Assembly's **Declaration of Intent for Change** was more than a simple statement of grievances. It was a bold proclamation of a new vision for France, one rooted in principles of equality, justice, and representation. As the representatives of the Third Estate convened in their new assembly, they recognized that symbolic gestures would not be enough. They needed to articulate a clear and transformative agenda, one that would challenge the existing order and lay the groundwork for a reformed nation. This declaration went far beyond addressing immediate issues; it aimed to redefine the relationship between the people and their government.

The declaration began by outlining the **fundamental inequalities** that had driven the Third Estate to form the National Assembly. The representatives addressed the oppressive tax burden that fell almost exclusively on the commoners, while the nobility and clergy enjoyed exemptions. They condemned the feudal dues that kept peasants in a cycle of poverty, bound to land they could never truly own. These grievances were not new, but the National Assembly's declaration gave them a powerful and unified voice, backed by the authority of the people's representatives. By highlighting these injustices, the assembly sent a message to the monarchy and the privileged estates that the people would no longer tolerate a system that exploited them.

The **vision of a new France** articulated in the declaration was grounded in Enlightenment ideals. The assembly drew on the writings of thinkers like Rousseau and Montesquieu, who argued for government based on the consent of the governed and a system of checks and balances. The declaration rejected the notion of absolute monarchy, asserting instead that the power of the government must come from the people. This was a radical departure from the Ancien Régime's belief in divine right, where the king ruled by God's will rather than by the will of the people. The National Assembly's declaration turned this idea on its head, insisting that sovereignty lay with the nation, not the monarch.

In their declaration, the assembly also emphasized the importance of **individual rights and freedoms**. They argued that every citizen was entitled to certain basic rights, including freedom of speech, freedom of assembly, and protection from arbitrary arrest. These principles were inspired by the Enlightenment's focus on individual liberty, as well as by the recent example of the American Revolution. The assembly's commitment to these rights resonated deeply with the people of France, who had long suffered under the weight of censorship, surveillance, and a judicial system that favored the powerful. By prioritizing these freedoms, the National Assembly signaled that the government's role was to protect its citizens, not to oppress them.

The declaration's call for **representation and accountability** marked a direct challenge to the monarchy's unchecked power. The assembly demanded a government where representatives would be elected by the people and answerable to them. This was a stark contrast to the Ancien Régime, where most decisions were made by the king and his advisors, with little input from the public. The idea that leaders should serve the people rather than their own interests was revolutionary in itself, and it reflected the growing sentiment that the monarchy had failed in its duty to protect and support the nation. By insisting on accountable governance, the National Assembly set a precedent for democratic principles that would later shape modern France.

The Declaration of Intent for Change also addressed the **role of the Church in French society**. The assembly called for a separation between church and state, arguing that religious institutions should not hold political power. This proposal was controversial, as the Church had long been intertwined with the monarchy, holding vast wealth and influence. However, many representatives believed that the Church's privileges were a barrier to equality and that its influence over public life needed to be curbed. By advocating for secular governance, the assembly sought to ensure that the state would serve all citizens equally, regardless of religious affiliation.

In outlining these principles, the National Assembly's declaration was not only a **blueprint for reform** but a call to action. It was a bold promise to the people of France that the old system would be replaced by one that respected their rights, addressed their needs, and represented their interests. This declaration was both a rejection of the past and an optimistic vision for the future, capturing the spirit of the Revolution and the desire for a fairer, more just society. It would serve as a guiding document, inspiring the people of France to believe in the possibility of a new era built on principles of equality, liberty, and solidarity.

The Role of Key Leaders

During the formation of the National Assembly and the events surrounding the **Tennis Court Oath**, several key leaders emerged whose actions and vision significantly shaped the early course of the French Revolution. These individuals were instrumental in pushing the Third Estate's demands forward, challenging the established order, and giving a face to the movement for political reform. They were not just representatives; they became symbols of defiance and determination, inspiring others to rally behind the revolutionary cause.

One of the most influential figures in the National Assembly was **Emmanuel-Joseph Sieyès**, a clergyman and political thinker whose pamphlet, *What is the Third Estate?*, had already stirred significant interest and controversy. In this pamphlet, Sieyès argued that the Third Estate was the true embodiment of the nation, declaring that they should not simply serve as an auxiliary to the nobility and clergy but should be the principal source of sovereignty. His ideas provided a philosophical foundation for the creation of the National Assembly and gave members of the Third Estate a strong sense of legitimacy. Sieyès urged the Third Estate to act independently when their demands for fair representation were ignored, and his calls for bold action helped guide them to the historic step of forming the National Assembly.

Another prominent leader during this period was **Honoré Gabriel Riqueti, the Comte de Mirabeau**, a charismatic and eloquent speaker whose background as a noble made his support for the Third Estate particularly striking. Mirabeau had long advocated for reform and was well known for his critical stance toward the monarchy. He quickly emerged as a leader in the assembly, urging moderation but also fierce determination. When the National Assembly was faced with opposition from the king and threats of being dissolved, Mirabeau famously declared, "We are here by the will of the people, and we will only be dispersed by the force of bayonets." His defiant stance underscored the assembly's resolve and helped unite its members against the king's attempts to undermine their authority. Mirabeau's speeches, delivered with passion and conviction, strengthened the National Assembly's commitment to their cause and inspired representatives to resist royal intimidation.

Jean-Sylvain Bailly, an astronomer and the elected president of the Third Estate, had a key organizational role. Bailly's calm and steady leadership helped to maintain order during tense moments, especially as frustrations mounted over the king's refusal to address the Third Estate's demands. Bailly presided over the gathering that ultimately led to the Tennis Court Oath, ensuring that the assembly's proceedings remained disciplined and focused. His commitment to the assembly's mission lent a sense of legitimacy to their actions, and he became a respected figure who symbolized the reasoned yet unyielding nature of the revolutionary movement. As the presiding officer, Bailly kept the assembly united, particularly during the symbolic act of the Tennis Court Oath, marking him as an essential leader in these critical early days.

The Marquis de Lafayette, already a national hero for his role in the American Revolution, brought his prestige and revolutionary credentials to the National Assembly. Although not as directly involved in the Tennis Court Oath itself, Lafayette was an outspoken advocate for constitutional reform and the rights of the people. His popularity and reputation lent further credibility to the assembly, and his influence would continue to grow in the months that followed. As a symbol of revolutionary ideals, Lafayette's presence reassured many that the assembly was pursuing a legitimate and honorable cause. He represented a bridge between the ideals of the American Revolution and the aspirations of the French people, and his support for reform signaled to the nobility and the military that the revolutionaries had allies among even the most respected members of society.

These leaders, with their varied backgrounds and approaches, unified the assembly and gave it both moral and strategic direction. Their words and actions encouraged representatives to push beyond the immediate demands of the Estates-General and envision a transformed France, laying the foundations for a revolutionary movement that would soon gain unstoppable momentum.

CHAPTER 4: STORMING THE BASTILLE

Symbolism of the Bastille

The **Bastille** was more than just a fortress; it was a towering symbol of the monarchy's absolute power and oppressive control over the people of France. For many Parisians, the Bastille represented the king's authority to imprison anyone without trial, based on the infamous *lettres de cachet*—sealed orders from the king that could sentence a person to prison without any due process. Over the years, stories circulated of individuals languishing in the Bastille's dark, cramped cells for petty offenses or as a result of political vendettas. Although these stories were sometimes exaggerated, they fueled a growing hatred for the Bastille and everything it represented.

The imposing architecture of the Bastille itself spoke volumes about the nature of royal power. With its thick stone walls, eight massive towers, and deep, shadowed dungeons, the Bastille was designed to be impenetrable. It loomed over a working-class neighborhood in Paris, a constant reminder to ordinary citizens that the monarchy held power over every aspect of their lives. People saw it every day, a looming fortress in their own city, and it reminded them of the monarchy's capacity for arbitrary and unchecked authority. For Parisians, the Bastille wasn't just a building; it was a physical manifestation of tyranny.

Despite its powerful reputation, the Bastille was no longer of great strategic importance by the late 1700s. The fortress housed only a handful of prisoners by 1789, including forgers and a few political prisoners whose crimes were not severe. Yet, the symbolism of the Bastille had far more weight than the reality of its current use. It had become a cultural icon of the Ancien Régime's injustices. Every citizen who walked by it felt the weight of royal oppression, seeing the fortress as an embodiment of everything wrong with the existing social and political order. The people's frustration and anger over years of economic hardship and political exclusion found a visible target in the Bastille.

The **storming of the Bastille** on July 14, 1789, turned this symbolism into revolutionary action. Word had spread that the fortress held a cache of gunpowder and arms, and with the city on edge, thousands of Parisians, fearing a crackdown by royal forces, gathered at its gates. The decision to storm the Bastille wasn't simply about seizing weapons; it was a deliberate act against the symbols of tyranny. People came with makeshift weapons, determination, and a willingness to face death, knowing that attacking the Bastille was an act of defiance against the king's authority. This wasn't a mere raid; it was a statement that the people would no longer live in fear of arbitrary imprisonment or repression.

The capture of the Bastille was a transformative moment. For the people of Paris and all of France, it represented a victory over despotism. When the fortress finally fell and its governor, Bernard-René de Launay, was captured, the citizens paraded his severed head on a pike through the streets. This gruesome display was a visceral message to the monarchy and the nobility: the people of France were no longer subjects who would meekly accept injustice. The symbolism of tearing down the Bastille went beyond the act itself—it was a declaration that they were prepared to dismantle the structures of oppression, piece by piece.

The **destruction of the Bastille** continued for days. Citizens tore it down brick by brick, taking fragments home as souvenirs, physical pieces of the fallen monarchy. The act of dismantling it themselves was powerful. This wasn't a top-down reform ordered by the king; it was the people claiming agency, erasing the symbol of tyranny with their own hands. The destruction of the fortress marked the end of a psychological barrier. The people felt empowered, realizing they could challenge and dismantle the systems that had oppressed them for so long.

After its fall, the Bastille quickly became an enduring symbol of the Revolution. It represented the people's unity and power, as well as their determination to overthrow a government that had ignored their cries for justice. Artists, writers, and revolutionaries celebrated the event in paintings, pamphlets, and speeches, turning the fall of the Bastille into a revolutionary icon. July 14 became a national celebration, honoring not only the physical act of storming the fortress but the spirit of resistance that it represented. The Bastille had gone from being a symbol of fear to a symbol of liberation.

The symbolism of the Bastille extended beyond France. News of its fall spread across Europe and inspired other movements against absolutist rulers. In countries where monarchies still wielded unchecked power, the fall of the Bastille signaled that change was possible, that ordinary people could rise up and challenge even the most entrenched systems. For revolutionary leaders outside France, the storming of the Bastille served as a rallying point, a vivid example of popular power overthrowing oppression. The fortress that once symbolized the monarchy's might became, instead, a powerful emblem of the people's resilience and collective strength.

In the context of the Revolution itself, the storming of the Bastille was a **unifying event**. People from all walks of life came together to participate in and celebrate the fall of the fortress. It was a moment that blurred social and class boundaries, as both the urban poor and members of the bourgeoisie found common cause in resisting tyranny. This unity was essential in building the revolutionary momentum that would soon lead to sweeping reforms and the eventual downfall of the monarchy. The fall of the Bastille showed that when united, the people could overcome any obstacle, no matter how imposing.

For the **royal family and the nobility**, the fall of the Bastille was a terrifying sign. It was a brutal reminder that the old order was crumbling and that the king's authority could no longer go unchallenged. The monarchy's response to the storming—half-hearted attempts to placate the people while reinforcing security—showed just how out of touch the ruling elite had become. They saw the event as an isolated outburst, failing to recognize it as a turning point that marked the beginning of a nationwide movement.

In every sense, the Bastille was more than a fortress; it was the most potent symbol of the French Revolution. Its fall was not just the beginning of the Revolution; it was the people's first real victory over oppression, a visible act of rebellion that signaled the start of a new era.

Events Leading to the Storming

The **events leading up to the Storming of the Bastille** were marked by growing anger, economic hardship, and rising tensions in Paris. By mid-1789, France was teetering on the edge of revolution. Years of financial mismanagement and deep social inequalities had created a powder keg, and the frustration of the Third Estate —the commoners—was at a breaking point. The Estates-General, called by King Louis XVI to address the financial crisis, had instead become the backdrop for a dramatic challenge to the existing order. When the Third Estate declared itself the National Assembly in June 1789, they took the first step toward a new political order. But this declaration was only the beginning; the situation in Paris would soon escalate toward violence.

Economic hardship was one of the primary forces pushing the people toward action. The 1780s had been marked by poor harvests, which drove up the price of bread, a staple of the French diet. By 1789, the cost of bread consumed most of a working-class family's income, leaving little left over for other necessities. Hunger was widespread, and **anger grew as people blamed the monarchy and the nobility for their suffering**. The luxurious lifestyle of the royal family and the nobility seemed to mock the struggles of the common people. The visible wealth of Versailles stood in stark contrast to the dire poverty many Parisians experienced, and the resentment simmered.

The **financial crisis that led to the Estates-General's assembly** was also a key factor. France was deeply in debt from years of expensive wars, including support for the American Revolution, and the state was on the verge of bankruptcy. The monarchy's efforts to raise taxes on the commoners had only deepened discontent, and when the king called the Estates-General, many hoped for significant reform. However, the rigid structure of the Estates-General, where each estate had only one vote, meant that the Third Estate was consistently outvoted by the First and Second Estates, the clergy and nobility. This unfair voting system effectively silenced the majority of France's population and underscored the lack of political power held by the common people.

The **formation of the National Assembly** was a direct response to this injustice. On June 17, 1789, the Third Estate, frustrated with their lack of influence, declared themselves the National Assembly, claiming to represent the will of the French people. This bold move was seen as an act of defiance against the monarchy and the privileged estates, and it was the first real indication that the Third Estate was ready to challenge the old order. The members of the National Assembly took the **Tennis Court Oath** on June 20, vowing not to disband until they had written a new constitution for France. This act of unity and resolve sent a powerful message that the people would not back down.

As the National Assembly continued to meet, **Louis XVI's response heightened the tension**. The king initially tried to ignore the Assembly's actions, but as its influence grew, he felt threatened. On June 23, he held a royal session, where he declared the Assembly's actions illegal and ordered them to disband. However, the deputies of the Third Estate refused to leave, demonstrating their commitment to change. Louis XVI then attempted a conciliatory approach by merging the three estates into a single assembly, but the trust between the monarchy and the people had already eroded. Many suspected that the king was only trying to buy time to reassert his authority.

Adding to the unease, **Louis XVI began to gather troops around Paris and Versailles**. By early July, nearly 20,000 royal soldiers were stationed in and around the capital. While the official explanation was that they were there to maintain order, many Parisians saw this as a show of force intended to intimidate the National Assembly and suppress any unrest. The people of Paris were already on edge, and the presence of troops only intensified their fears. Rumors circulated that the king planned to dissolve the Assembly by force, arrest its leaders, and crack down on any opposition. This perceived threat from the monarchy increased the urgency among Parisians to take matters into their own hands.

The **dismissal of Jacques Necker**, the popular finance minister, on July 11, was the final spark. Necker was seen as a reformer sympathetic to the people's grievances, and his efforts to stabilize the economy had earned him support among the Third Estate and the public. When the king dismissed Necker, it was viewed as a sign that he was abandoning any pretense of reform and was preparing to take a hardline stance against the National Assembly and the people's demands. News of Necker's dismissal spread quickly through Paris, fueling anger and resentment. Crowds began to gather, and demonstrations erupted in the streets. Necker's dismissal symbolized to many that the monarchy was not interested in change and would use any means necessary to retain control.

As tensions reached a boiling point, **Parisians began to arm themselves**. They feared a military crackdown and believed they needed to defend the National Assembly and their right to reform. People looted gun shops, seizing weapons to protect themselves. Crowds assembled at the Hôtel des Invalides, a military hospital where weapons were stored, and managed to secure a cache of muskets. However, they lacked gunpowder, which led them to focus their attention on the **Bastille**, a fortress and prison that had long symbolized royal tyranny.

The **Bastille was more than just a prison**; it was a symbol of the king's absolute power. For years, the monarchy had used it to detain political prisoners without trial, making it a hated symbol of oppression. By 1789, the Bastille held only a handful of prisoners, but its presence loomed large in the minds of Parisians. The fortress was rumored to contain a significant supply of gunpowder, and seizing it would not only provide the people with the means to arm themselves but also send a powerful message of defiance to the monarchy. The Bastille represented the old order, and taking it would be a clear rejection of royal authority.

On the morning of **July 14, 1789**, a crowd gathered around the Bastille, demanding that the governor, Bernard-René de Launay, surrender the fortress and hand over its weapons and gunpowder. Negotiations were tense and drawn-out, with de Launay hesitant to yield to the crowd. As the discussions dragged on, the crowd grew restless. Some members of the crowd managed to break into the outer courtyard, and a firefight erupted between the guards and the people. The violence escalated quickly, with the crowd refusing to back down.

After hours of fighting, de Launay, realizing that he could no longer hold the Bastille, agreed to surrender. However, as he opened the gates, chaos broke out. The mob surged inside, capturing the guards and taking control of the fortress. In the aftermath, de Launay was killed by the crowd, and his head was paraded through the streets on a pike. The fall of the Bastille was a decisive moment; it marked the first time that the people had successfully challenged the monarchy with armed force. News of the Bastille's fall spread rapidly across France, inspiring uprisings in towns and villages where people began to rise up against feudal lords and demand change.

The **events leading to the Storming of the Bastille** showed the depth of popular anger and the extent to which people were willing to fight for their rights. The dismissal of Necker, the presence of troops in Paris, and the economic desperation all contributed to a sense that the monarchy was an obstacle to the well-being of the people. When the Bastille fell, it sent a clear message: the old ways of absolute power and feudal privilege could no longer withstand the will of the people. This moment shifted the Revolution into a new, more radical phase, where the people would have a central role in shaping France's future.

Aftermath and Public Response

The **aftermath of the Bastille's fall** sent shockwaves through Paris and across France. Word of the successful storming spread rapidly, and citizens from all social backgrounds celebrated what they saw as a triumph over oppression. The fall of the Bastille became an instant symbol of the people's ability to stand against tyranny, inspiring others to join the revolutionary cause. Crowds paraded through the streets, carrying pieces of the Bastille's demolished walls as trophies. For the people of

Paris, it was more than just a military victory; it was a validation of their strength and determination to resist the monarchy's oppression.

Parisians immediately began **demolishing the Bastille**, tearing it down brick by brick. This act was both practical and symbolic. They dismantled the fortress as if erasing a stain on their city, turning pieces of its walls into mementos. Merchants and artisans took small chunks of stone to sell or keep as personal symbols of freedom. The destruction of the Bastille continued over several days, with workers and commoners taking pride in the act of physically removing the structure that had once cast a shadow over their lives. The fortress that had represented repression was now being reduced to rubble by the very people it had once threatened.

The public's response went beyond celebration and physical destruction; **the fall of the Bastille also triggered widespread political action**. Local revolutionary groups, known as "communes," began forming in neighborhoods throughout Paris, organizing to address the people's needs and coordinate responses to the changing political landscape. These communes empowered citizens who had never before held any influence over governance, creating a sense of participation and agency. Citizens felt a newfound responsibility to contribute to the future of France, and these small political bodies would soon play crucial roles in directing revolutionary events in Paris.

The **news of the Bastille's fall reached King Louis XVI** with a harsh impact. On July 15, he reportedly asked, "Is it a revolt?" to which the Duke of La Rochefoucauld famously replied, "No, Sire, it is a revolution." For the king and his advisors, the fall of the Bastille was a wake-up call, revealing the full extent of the people's anger and resolve. Louis XVI, shaken by the uprising, withdrew his troops from Paris, recognizing that a direct confrontation with the people could further destabilize his reign. This retreat marked a significant shift in power, as the king's loss of control over Paris sent a message to the entire nation that the monarchy's authority was now vulnerable.

In the weeks following the Bastille's fall, the **people of France began to challenge other symbols of royal authority**. Inspired by the events in Paris, towns and villages across the country saw similar uprisings, as citizens stormed local fortresses, seized weapons, and formed their own militias. Rural peasants, too, felt emboldened by the news, leading to widespread attacks on noble estates in what would become known as the "Great Fear." The Bastille's fall ignited a wave of revolutionary activity that rippled outward, bringing the spirit of defiance to every corner of France.

Public response also included an outpouring of **creative expressions**, as artists, writers, and pamphleteers celebrated the Bastille's destruction. They produced paintings, engravings, and poems that commemorated the day's events, depicting the storming as a heroic and transformative act. These artworks became immensely popular, spreading the image of the fall of the Bastille to those who hadn't witnessed it firsthand. The creative responses further solidified the storming of the

Bastille as a pivotal moment in the collective memory of France, inspiring even those outside Paris to view the Revolution as a righteous struggle for freedom.

The aftermath of the Bastille's storming also brought **new political figures to prominence**. Leaders of the revolution emerged, taking on roles within the National Assembly and the growing network of communes. Figures like Camille Desmoulins, who had rallied Parisians just days before, gained popular support, while others took on influential roles within the newly formed revolutionary government in Paris. The fall of the Bastille set the stage for a new political order, one where the people held power, and it paved the way for emerging leaders to take bold action on behalf of the people.

For the people of Paris, the storming of the Bastille was a clear message: they had both the right and the power to demand change.

CHAPTER 5: THE GREAT FEAR AND RURAL REVOLTS

Peasant Uprisings and Rebellion

The **peasant uprisings** that erupted in the summer of 1789 during what became known as the Great Fear were some of the most intense and widespread episodes of unrest in the French countryside. News of the fall of the Bastille in Paris had electrified the nation, and peasants across France, who had long endured the burdens of feudal dues, high taxes, and exploitation, saw a window for change. They seized this moment of chaos to confront their landlords, seeking not only relief from their daily suffering but also a symbolic overthrow of a centuries-old system that had kept them bound to the land and in debt.

In rural France, life had been harsh for generations. Peasants faced relentless obligations that forced them to pay dues to the nobility, work unpaid on their landlords' land, and pay taxes to the Church and the monarchy. These feudal dues, or *corvées*, kept many peasants impoverished and dependent. Any small crisis, whether a poor harvest or rising food prices, could tip families into starvation. As economic conditions worsened in the 1780s, fueled by bad harvests and increasing debt, frustration in the countryside mounted. The arrival of news from Paris that the people had risen up against symbols of oppression, like the Bastille, set off a spark among peasants who had been waiting for a chance to break free from their own chains.

As rumors spread that **bands of brigands** were moving through the countryside, allegedly sent by nobles to punish rebellious peasants, fear quickly took hold. Villagers armed themselves, preparing to defend their families and land. But in many areas, these rumors of brigands morphed into a justification for direct action. Peasants, already fearful and on edge, began organizing into groups and targeting symbols of their oppression. They stormed manor houses, often with makeshift weapons, tearing through records and documents that listed their obligations and debts. Destroying these records was an act of liberation; by eliminating these symbols of feudalism, they believed they could free themselves from the system that had kept them in poverty.

The attacks were not random acts of violence. They were **targeted acts of rebellion** against the structures of feudal power. Peasants aimed their fury at the physical and symbolic representations of noble privilege: grain stores, estates, and especially **feudal records**. These records, often meticulously kept by landlords, detailed every tax, tithe, and corvée that peasants owed. By destroying them, peasants were not only venting their anger but also taking a practical step to cancel their debts and obligations. In some cases, entire families joined these uprisings, knowing that they were risking their lives to achieve even the chance of freedom from their crushing burdens.

These uprisings also became an outlet for long-simmering grievances against **local landlords**, who often treated peasants with indifference or outright cruelty. Many nobles lived far from the estates they controlled, paying little attention to the lives of the peasants who worked their land. Others lived lavishly while peasants struggled to survive. This disconnect fed a deep resentment that exploded during the Great Fear. Peasants saw the landlords as symbols of everything wrong with their lives: they represented the wealth, privilege, and cruelty that had denied common people a chance at dignity. By storming their estates, peasants were not just rebelling against individuals; they were rebelling against an entire system that dehumanized them.

Some nobles were caught off-guard by the intensity of the peasants' actions. While a few tried to defend their estates, others fled at the first sign of rebellion, leaving behind properties that were quickly looted or set ablaze. In certain regions, peasants would parade through villages with pieces of burned manor houses or feudal documents, using these items as trophies of their newfound power. This was more than destruction—it was a statement of independence, an announcement that they would no longer accept lives governed by feudal rules.

In some cases, peasants seized **grain and food supplies** stored on noble estates. For people who had faced hunger and hardship for years, taking control of these resources was a direct solution to their immediate needs. Grain was the staple of the French diet, and access to food had always been limited by the taxes imposed by landlords. By reclaiming these stores, peasants saw themselves as rectifying the injustices that had kept them perpetually hungry. In towns and villages, locals often distributed the grain among themselves, creating a sense of communal victory over the old system of scarcity and dependence.

The **spread of the Great Fear** reflected the profound unity among the peasants, as word of one village's uprising quickly traveled to others. People saw what was possible when they stood together, and a chain reaction of revolts swept across France. Villagers would receive news of uprisings in nearby regions, and emboldened by these stories, they would take up arms against their own landlords. This wave of rebellion turned into a powerful movement, where peasants felt empowered by the collective actions of others facing similar struggles.

However, these uprisings were not universally embraced. Some local officials and even members of the National Assembly were alarmed by the extent of the violence in the countryside. They feared that the peasant revolts would destabilize the nation further and undermine the cause of the Revolution itself. Nevertheless, the National Assembly recognized that the peasants' grievances were legitimate, and it could not ignore the cries of the rural population, especially as the assembly relied on popular support to pursue its own reforms. These uprisings demonstrated that the momentum for change was not limited to Paris or the urban bourgeoisie—it was a national movement driven by people across all regions and classes.

The **enduring impact of the peasant revolts** became clear when the National Assembly passed the August Decrees in response to the Great Fear. These decrees abolished feudal privileges and dues, acknowledging that the feudal system could no longer continue. The actions of the peasants in tearing down their own bonds of servitude had forced the assembly to confront the reality that France's social structure was fundamentally broken. By pushing the National Assembly to dismantle the system of feudal obligations, the peasant uprisings showed that the Revolution was not only about political power but about transforming society from the ground up.

The Great Fear was, at its heart, a rebellion against a lifetime of oppression, poverty, and injustice. For peasants who had labored under feudal constraints for generations, this moment represented a rare and exhilarating opportunity to break free. They knew the risks of confronting the nobility, but for them, the potential reward—a life without feudal dues and arbitrary control—was worth the danger. These uprisings sent a clear message: the people of France would no longer live as subjects to a system that denied them agency and dignity.

Spread of Fear and Panic Across France

The **Great Fear** swept across rural France in the summer of 1789, a wave of panic and violence that shook the countryside just as the Revolution was gathering momentum in Paris. The fear spread rapidly and unpredictably, igniting peasant uprisings and deepening the social turmoil that gripped France. This panic stemmed from a mixture of rumors, mistrust, and long-standing resentment against the nobility. While Paris had its moment of upheaval with the Storming of the Bastille, the countryside experienced its own form of rebellion, one fueled by fears that the old feudal order was attempting to reassert control and crush the hopes for change.

The **spread of fear across rural France began with rumors**. News traveled slowly in 18th-century France, and reliable information was often hard to come by. This environment made the countryside ripe for misinformation, and by the summer of 1789, rumors were spreading that bands of armed brigands, possibly sent by nobles or even foreign mercenaries, were attacking villages and destroying crops. The rumors varied, but they shared a common theme: that the aristocracy was conspiring to take revenge on the peasants for supporting the Revolution. In some accounts, it was said that nobles were hiring mercenaries to crush any resistance to the feudal system. In others, the fear was that foreign soldiers were coming to support the monarchy and restore the old order.

For rural peasants, who were already facing severe economic hardships, these rumors fed into an existing sense of **insecurity and vulnerability**. The high price of bread, poor harvests, and oppressive feudal dues had already created a desperate situation. The thought of roaming bands of brigands, allegedly acting on behalf of the nobility, threatened to plunge them even further into poverty and hunger. People began to arm themselves with whatever weapons they could find, preparing to defend their homes and fields. Even though these bands of brigands largely existed only in the minds of the fearful, the preparations for defense were very real.

The **panic spread through local networks of communication**—traveling merchants, messengers, and even the clergy passed along tales of attacks and impending violence. News of the events in Paris, including the fall of the Bastille, reached the countryside around the same time, intensifying the sense of unrest. While the Parisians had risen up against the monarchy, many peasants felt that they, too, were on the verge of confrontation, though theirs was with the local aristocracy rather than the distant king. Each town and village received and reshaped the rumors, adapting them to local contexts and fears, making the panic unpredictable and hard to control.

This **panic soon transformed into a movement of resistance and retaliation**. Convinced that they were about to be attacked, peasants took preemptive action. They banded together to protect their communities, sometimes forming militias to guard against the rumored brigands. But as the days passed and no attackers appeared, their anger shifted from imagined threats to very real local grievances. Peasants began targeting the symbols of feudal authority, ransacking manors, burning records of dues and debts, and seizing land. These records, often kept in manor houses, documented the taxes and services owed by the peasants to the lords. Destroying these documents was a way of freeing themselves from the obligations of feudalism.

In some areas, **entire estates were overrun** as peasants stormed the homes of their landlords. They took whatever they could, sometimes to sell, but often to make a point. It was an act of defiance against the nobility that had controlled their lives for so long. Many lords fled from their estates, fearing for their safety, and those who stayed sometimes faced direct confrontations with the peasants. Though violence varied in intensity, the peasants made their anger known through destruction and demands for relief from feudal dues. They were no longer willing to submit to the authority of the local aristocrats, and the Great Fear became a grassroots revolt against the entire system of feudal oppression.

This spread of **fear and rebellion wasn't limited to any one region**. It touched nearly every part of France, from the northern plains to the southern hills, as peasants everywhere shared similar grievances and frustrations. Each community responded in its own way, but the overarching theme was consistent: a deep-seated rage against feudal dues, a desire for freedom from the nobility, and a determination to assert control over their lives. This widespread unrest demonstrated how deeply the Revolution's ideals had penetrated into rural France, where people were ready to fight for their own rights and dignity.

The **response from the National Assembly in Paris** was initially slow, as the Assembly was caught off guard by the scale and intensity of the rural uprisings. However, as reports flooded in, the Assembly realized the need to address the peasants' grievances to prevent the situation from spiraling further out of control. On August 4, 1789, the Assembly took a dramatic step by issuing the **August**

Decrees, which abolished feudal privileges and removed many of the dues and obligations that had burdened the peasants. The Decrees were an attempt to appease the peasants and bring an end to the violence, acknowledging that the old feudal structures could no longer hold.

The Great Fear and the spread of panic across France showed the depth of **resentment against the feudal system** and the extent to which people were willing to rise up for change. It wasn't just about protecting themselves from imagined threats; it was an assertion of power by the rural population, a demand to be freed from the chains of feudal obligations. The fear that spread across France became a catalyst for dismantling the feudal system, pushing the Revolution further toward radical change and reinforcing the idea that sovereignty rested with the people, not with the nobility or the king.

Rural Revolts and Attack on Feudal Symbols

As word of the events in Paris reached rural villages, peasants across France grew emboldened, taking up arms and directing their fury at the symbols of feudal oppression. This was more than just a reaction to specific grievances—it was a deep-seated rebellion against centuries of exploitation. The feudal system, with its lords and noble privileges, had long extracted labor, dues, and respect from the rural peasantry, and now those symbols of power became targets of a popular uprising. The peasants seized the moment to assert their autonomy, challenging not only their local lords but also the structure of feudalism itself.

The **targets of the rural revolts were not random**; they were precise and symbolic. Peasants aimed their attacks at the physical embodiments of feudal power: the manor houses, the châteaux of the nobility, and the feudal records that documented their obligations. Manor houses were often the largest and most prominent buildings in a village, representing the authority of the lord who ruled over the local population. These buildings housed not only the noble families but also the records that kept the peasants bound to centuries-old dues and labor obligations. For many, destroying these records was as important as destroying the manor itself. By burning the feudal documents, peasants sought to erase the paper trail of their servitude, severing ties to the oppressive system that had controlled their lives.

The **feudal records were a primary target** because they held a tangible link to the system of dues and labor requirements that burdened the peasantry. These records listed the specific duties, taxes, and fees each family owed, documenting debts that were often impossible to escape. A typical peasant family might owe a variety of payments: rents for their land, a share of their harvests, and even fees for using local resources like mills and ovens, which were owned by the lord. These dues weighed heavily on the rural population, especially during times of poor harvests or economic downturns. To the peasants, these documents were a constant reminder of their subjugation, and destroying them became a powerful act of defiance.

In many areas, **peasants stormed the manors and châteaux**, sometimes forcing their way in with makeshift weapons, and demanded that lords hand over the feudal registers. In some cases, the lords fled in anticipation of the peasants' arrival, abandoning their estates to avoid confrontation. Those who remained faced the wrath of a population that had reached its limit. It was common for peasants to drag out and burn the feudal records in public bonfires, symbolizing the destruction of their ties to their feudal obligations. This act was not just a matter of practical relief from debts; it was deeply symbolic, a rejection of the entire system that had kept them bound to servitude.

The **manor house itself became a symbol to be attacked**. Many peasants looted or destroyed these grand residences, stripping them of valuables and tearing down structures that symbolized nobility's dominance. For generations, the manor had been a place of authority where the lord collected taxes, dispensed justice, and enforced feudal obligations. Peasants who had spent their lives bowing before these figures now took back the power by entering these forbidden spaces, taking whatever they could, and asserting their own rights. Some villagers even occupied the manors, transforming them into gathering places where they discussed the new ideas of the Revolution and the possibilities of a future without feudal oppression.

The **attacks on feudal symbols varied by region** but were widespread, touching nearly every corner of France. In the eastern provinces, where feudalism was particularly harsh, peasants rose up with exceptional intensity. In these areas, the obligations imposed on peasants were among the most severe in France, including requirements to work specific days for the lord, provide a portion of their crops, and pay fees that left them barely able to survive. The harshness of these conditions meant that when the opportunity to rebel arose, peasants seized it with a vengeance. They were not just protesting taxes; they were revolting against the feudal lifestyle that had controlled every aspect of their existence.

The **violence of these rural revolts shocked the aristocracy**, who saw their authority slipping away. Many noble families, seeing the spread of attacks on manors and the destruction of feudal records, fled to Paris or even left France altogether. These **émigrés** became a growing population of exiled nobility who looked for support from foreign monarchies to restore their lost power. The rural revolts and the Great Fear fueled their narrative that the Revolution was spiraling out of control, feeding into their pleas for foreign intervention. This exodus of nobles not only left their estates unguarded but also accelerated the collapse of feudal authority in the countryside, as many lords abandoned their lands, leaving the peasantry in control.

In some areas, **peasants took their actions even further**, targeting not only the local lords but also the infrastructure that maintained the feudal economy. Mills, which were often controlled by the lord and required peasants to pay fees to grind their grain, were attacked. Forests, which peasants had limited access to despite their reliance on wood for fuel and building materials, were seized. The revolt against feudal symbols extended beyond the manors to the systems and resources that sustained the lords' power. This showed the peasants' understanding that to dismantle feudalism, they had to go beyond symbolic attacks and disrupt the economic structures that upheld it.

The **National Assembly in Paris watched these events unfold with growing concern**. The rural revolts, while expressing popular anger, threatened to destabilize the Revolution and turn public opinion against the Assembly. In response to the widespread destruction and social upheaval, the Assembly passed the **August Decrees** on August 4, 1789. As we'll cover more in the next chapter, these decrees effectively abolished feudal privileges, ending the dues and obligations that had been a central part of rural life under the Ancien Régime. By formally ending feudal rights, the Assembly hoped to bring order to the countryside and calm the unrest that threatened to spread even further. It was a monumental shift, marking the end of feudalism in France and signaling that the Revolution was on the side of the common people.

The rural revolts and the attack on feudal symbols were more than just expressions of anger; they were acts of reclamation. The peasants were reclaiming their dignity, their labor, and their right to exist without the oppressive weight of feudalism. They seized the moment of revolutionary change to assert their role in shaping a new France. The destruction of feudal symbols was a powerful demonstration that the old social order, built on hierarchy and privilege, was crumbling. These actions paved the way for a society where the people, not the nobility, held power. The rural revolts forced the Revolution to move forward and align itself with the peasants' call for a fairer, freer existence.

CHAPTER 6: ABOLITION OF FEUDAL PRIVILEGES

The August Decrees

The **August Decrees**, issued by the National Assembly in August 1789, marked a profound shift in French society, dismantling the centuries-old system of feudal privileges that had defined life in the Ancien Régime. These decrees didn't just announce reforms; they signaled a radical transformation, stripping the nobility and clergy of their special rights and opening the door to a society based on equality and merit rather than birth and privilege. The decrees were a response to the widespread unrest and violence in the countryside during the Great Fear, where peasants had taken matters into their own hands, attacking manors and burning records that symbolized their oppression. Faced with this upheaval, the National Assembly saw the need for immediate action to calm the chaos and address the grievances fueling these revolts.

On the night of August 4, the National Assembly gathered in an urgent session, where a remarkable scene unfolded. Members of the nobility and clergy stood up, one after another, to renounce their own privileges in a spontaneous and symbolic gesture of unity. Noblemen, who had been accustomed to special rights since birth, declared that they would give up their tax exemptions, hunting rights, and seigneurial dues. Bishops and priests offered to forgo the tithes that had enriched the Church for centuries. The atmosphere was electric, as representatives cast off the very privileges that had separated them from the common people. This moment, known as the **"Night of August 4,"** was revolutionary in itself, as it showed a willingness, at least among some members of the privileged classes, to break from the structures of the past.

The following day, the National Assembly translated these symbolic gestures into **formal legislation** with the August Decrees. These decrees targeted the core features of feudalism. The first and perhaps most important decree abolished feudal dues and obligations, the payments and services peasants had been forced to render to their lords in return for the right to live and work on the land. This step meant that peasants would no longer have to pay fees for using common lands or grinding grain in the lord's mill. By erasing these dues, the Assembly gave peasants a freedom they had never known, relieving them of the burdens that had kept them impoverished and dependent on the nobility.

Another key point in the decrees was the **elimination of seigneurial justice**, which had allowed local lords to serve as both landowners and judges over their tenants. Under the feudal system, lords had been empowered to oversee legal disputes on their estates, often judging cases in their own interests. This authority had long created an imbalance, as peasants knew they would rarely find justice in courts controlled by their landlords. With the August Decrees, the National

Assembly stripped lords of this power, shifting judicial authority to local and national courts that would, in theory, serve all citizens equally. This change was a monumental step toward creating a fair and impartial legal system.

The **abolition of tithes** was another significant element in the August Decrees. For centuries, peasants and commoners had been required to pay tithes, or a portion of their income, to the Church, which used these funds to support its clergy and maintain its vast wealth. Many viewed these tithes as an unjust tax that benefited the upper levels of the Church hierarchy while burdening those who could least afford it. By ending mandatory tithes, the Assembly struck at the Church's economic power, aligning itself with the widespread calls for a secular state. This decision also addressed the grievances of the rural poor, who saw the Church as yet another institution that enriched itself at their expense.

The **hunting rights** of the nobility, often resented by peasants, were also targeted in the August Decrees. Under feudal law, nobles held exclusive rights to hunt on certain lands, even if those lands were worked by peasants. This privilege was not just about hunting; it represented the aristocracy's dominance over both the land and those who lived on it. Nobles could trample crops, interrupt work, and generally interfere with the lives of peasants in pursuit of their sport. By eliminating these hunting rights, the Assembly sent a clear message that the land would no longer serve as a playground for the wealthy. This decree restored dignity to the peasantry, allowing them to work the land without fearing that their labor might be damaged by a passing noble's whim.

The August Decrees also tackled the issue of **tax equality**. Previously, the nobility and clergy had enjoyed exemptions from many taxes, leaving the burden on the Third Estate. The Assembly's decrees ended these exemptions, requiring all citizens, regardless of birth or title, to contribute to the state. This move was essential for both symbolic and practical reasons. Symbolically, it reinforced the idea that all citizens were equal before the law and the state. Practically, it meant that France could potentially build a more stable and equitable tax base to support its finances. By ending tax privileges, the Assembly was taking a crucial step toward financial reform, addressing one of the core economic injustices that had fueled revolutionary fervor.

These sweeping reforms of the August Decrees **redefined the social structure of France**. For centuries, French society had been organized into estates, with privileges and obligations tied to one's birth. The decrees cut through these layers of privilege, creating a framework in which all citizens would, theoretically, stand on equal ground. They shifted the focus from inherited status to individual citizenship, aligning the nation with Enlightenment ideals of equality and justice. This was a dramatic break from tradition, moving France away from a feudal society and toward a modern nation-state.

However, implementing these decrees was challenging. Many nobles resisted the loss of their privileges, especially in regions where they held significant local power. In some areas, they ignored the decrees entirely, refusing to give up their dues or honor the new laws. For peasants, the decrees offered hope but also raised questions about enforcement. In cases where local lords clung to their rights, peasants sometimes had to resort to further uprisings to assert the freedoms promised by the Assembly. This ongoing tension between the promises of the decrees and the realities on the ground underscored the depth of France's transformation and the obstacles it faced.

The August Decrees represented a critical turning point. They were the first major legal step in dismantling the feudal system and embodying the principles that had inspired the Revolution. By enshrining these changes into law, the National Assembly set a precedent for further reforms, sending a message that the Revolution would not merely modify the old order but create an entirely new society based on liberty, equality, and fraternity. The decrees may have started as a response to peasant revolts, but they ended as the foundation for a new vision of French citizenship.

End of Noble Privileges and Feudal Rights

The **abolition of feudal privileges** and the end of noble rights in France marked a radical shift from the entrenched inequalities that had defined the Ancien Régime. For centuries, the nobility had enjoyed a set of privileges that set them apart from the rest of society. These privileges went beyond wealth or property; they included legal rights and economic advantages that placed them above ordinary citizens. From exemption from most taxes to the right to collect feudal dues from peasants, the nobility's status was entrenched in law and tradition. But in August 1789, the National Assembly shattered this foundation, enacting the **August Decrees** to eliminate noble privileges and feudal rights, creating the groundwork for a society based on equality before the law.

One of the most immediate and significant changes was the **abolition of feudal dues**. This ended the requirement for peasants to pay fees to their landlords for basic rights, like using mills, ovens, and wine presses, which the nobility often controlled. These dues had been a constant drain on peasant incomes, forcing them to pay simply for access to tools and facilities essential for daily survival. The dues symbolized their dependence on the nobility, and their elimination freed the rural population from the last remnants of feudal subjugation. By removing these payments, the Assembly granted peasants a new economic autonomy, allowing them to keep more of their own earnings and, for the first time, to work the land for their own benefit.

The **elimination of noble hunting rights** was another revolutionary change. For generations, French nobles had exclusive hunting privileges on land, even if it was worked by peasants. This wasn't just about sport; it was about control. Nobles could trample crops, interrupt work, and even damage peasant property as they pursued their game, with no regard for the losses this might cause. By abolishing these rights, the Assembly symbolically returned ownership of the land to the people who worked it, ending the nobility's dominion over both land and labor. Peasants were now able to manage their fields without interference, a fundamental shift that offered them a new sense of independence.

The **end of seigneurial justice** was another key aspect of the August Decrees. Under the old system, nobles had the right to act as local judges on their estates, resolving disputes and enforcing laws within their domain. This arrangement was deeply biased, as nobles typically ruled in their own favor, leaving peasants with little hope for fair treatment. Seigneurial justice had not only reinforced the nobility's authority but also prevented peasants from accessing an impartial legal system. By eliminating this judicial power, the Assembly aimed to create a unified legal framework in which every citizen, regardless of social status, could expect equal treatment under the law. Justice was now in the hands of public courts, reducing the nobility's influence and laying the foundation for a fairer system.

Exemption from taxes was also targeted in the abolition of noble privileges. The nobility and clergy had long been exempt from many of the taxes that burdened the Third Estate, a situation that had contributed to widespread resentment and economic inequality. The Assembly's decrees required that all citizens, noble or common, contribute to the state's finances. This change was essential for establishing the principle that everyone, regardless of birth or title, shared in the responsibilities of the nation. Tax equality not only addressed a core grievance of the common people but also helped stabilize France's financial situation by expanding the tax base. With nobles now required to pay, the state had a more reliable source of revenue, lessening the dependence on taxes that had unfairly targeted the lower classes.

The **abolition of tithes** paid to the Church also struck at the heart of feudal society. Tithes were a mandatory portion of income that peasants and landowners had to pay to the Church, which used the funds to support clergy and religious institutions. By ending this system, the Assembly relieved peasants of yet another financial burden. It also signaled a shift toward secularism, as the Church's economic power was closely tied to its role in the feudal order. Removing the tithe reduced the clergy's influence and wealth, aligning with the Revolution's aim to separate religious authority from state affairs and reinforce the idea that citizens should support institutions voluntarily, not through forced contributions.

Each aspect of the feudal system that was abolished in the August Decrees represented a **break from the past**. The end of noble privileges and feudal rights did more than just improve the lives of peasants; it fundamentally altered the structure of French society. The abolition of these privileges meant that no individual could claim special treatment simply due to birth, shifting the focus from inherited status to citizenship. These changes helped create a sense of national identity, where all citizens, from noble to peasant, would be subject to the same laws and responsibilities, setting the stage for a society based on equality and justice.

Response from the Aristocracy and Clergy

The **aristocracy and clergy** reacted with shock and disbelief to the sudden and sweeping abolition of their privileges. Many of them had never anticipated such a drastic move from the National Assembly, even as tensions had escalated. For the nobility, their privileges were more than a set of rights; they were part of their identity, woven into the fabric of their lives. They viewed the August Decrees as a direct attack on the values and traditions that defined the Ancien Régime. The idea that feudal dues, exclusive rights, and seigneurial justice would be stripped away was, to them, an affront to the natural order.

Nobles in rural areas were particularly impacted, as they depended on **feudal dues** as a primary source of income. For many landlords, these dues were not just symbolic but practical, representing a steady revenue stream that supported their estates and lifestyles. Without these payments, many nobles found themselves facing financial difficulties, unable to sustain their properties and households. Some nobles who had inherited debt-ridden estates saw the end of dues as a financial disaster. The sudden loss of income led to bitterness and resentment, particularly among those who relied on their estates to sustain their wealth and standing.

The **abolition of seigneurial justice** also struck a nerve with the nobility. This judicial power had given them authority over their lands, reinforcing their dominance within local communities. To lose this right felt like a humiliation, as it forced them to submit to the same legal standards as commoners. Many nobles felt that this eroded their status, reducing them to mere landowners with no special role in governance. This loss of authority fostered a sense of betrayal among the nobility, who viewed the Assembly's actions as a degradation of their ancestral rights and responsibilities.

Among the clergy, especially the **higher-ranking bishops and abbots**, the abolition of tithes and privileges was deeply unsettling. The Church had long enjoyed both spiritual and economic power, supported by the wealth generated from tithes. Many clergy members depended on these funds to maintain their positions and estates, and they saw the removal of tithes as an attack on the Church's stability and role in society. Some bishops spoke out vehemently against the decrees, arguing that the Church had a divine right to these contributions and warning that the Assembly was leading France into moral decay by undermining religious institutions.

However, not all clergy members opposed the decrees. **Lower-ranking parish priests**, many of whom came from modest backgrounds, often sympathized with the people and understood the financial strain that tithes placed on peasant families. Some of these priests even voiced support for the abolition, seeing it as an opportunity to make the Church more accessible and focused on serving the spiritual needs of the poor. This internal division within the clergy weakened the

Church's opposition to the decrees, as not all members could unify against the changes imposed by the National Assembly.

In response to these upheavals, the **aristocracy began organizing resistance**, meeting in private gatherings to discuss strategies for preserving what remained of their influence. Many nobles fled to foreign countries, becoming known as émigrés, and began working to rally support against the Revolution. They reached out to other European monarchies, hoping to convince them to intervene in France and restore the old order. These exiled nobles viewed the Revolution as a dangerous experiment that threatened the stability of all European monarchies. The presence of émigrés working from abroad created a growing anxiety within France that outside forces might soon attempt to crush the revolutionary government.

Inside France, the nobility's resentment grew, especially as they watched their traditional status and influence fade. Some resisted openly, refusing to recognize the decrees and even attempting to enforce feudal dues in defiance of the new laws. This resistance was met with hostility from the public, who viewed such defiance as a refusal to accept the new principles of equality and justice. The response from the nobility and clergy reflected the deep divisions within French society as the Revolution sought to redefine social structures that had persisted for centuries.

CHAPTER 7: THE DECLARATION OF THE RIGHTS OF MAN AND CITIZEN

Drafting and Ideals of the Declaration

The **Declaration of the Rights of Man and Citizen**, drafted in August 1789, was a landmark document that laid out the ideals of the French Revolution. The National Assembly, filled with representatives from the Third Estate and inspired by Enlightenment thought, crafted the declaration to define the principles of a new society founded on liberty, equality, and individual rights. This document wasn't just a list of demands; it was a profound statement that redefined what it meant to be a citizen and outlined the fundamental rights owed to every individual by virtue of their humanity. For the first time in French history, the declaration asserted that rights were not granted by the king or derived from social status but were inherent to all people.

The drafting process involved intense debate. The National Assembly drew inspiration from the **Enlightenment philosophers**, whose ideas about human nature and government had circulated widely in the years leading up to the Revolution. Thinkers like Rousseau, Montesquieu, and Locke had argued for the concept of natural rights—rights that every person held simply by being human. Rousseau's ideas about the "social contract" and the sovereignty of the people influenced the assembly's approach to government. According to Rousseau, a legitimate government should be based on the consent of the governed, and authority must be derived from the people themselves. This concept underpinned the declaration, marking a complete break from the traditional idea that the king's authority was divinely appointed.

The assembly also looked to recent events, especially the **American Revolution** and its own Declaration of Independence, which had asserted the right to life, liberty, and the pursuit of happiness. The American example was particularly influential for figures like the Marquis de Lafayette, who had fought in the American Revolution and were essential in drafting the French declaration. Lafayette, along with other progressive members of the Assembly, pushed to include universal principles that would ensure individual freedoms and limit the powers of government. They wanted a document that would resonate not only within France but across the world, showcasing France's commitment to freedom and equality.

Liberty was a central ideal in the Declaration. Article 1 declared that "Men are born and remain free and equal in rights," a powerful statement that challenged the centuries-old class distinctions of the Ancien Régime. This simple yet revolutionary line established equality as a foundational principle of the new society, rejecting the privileges that had previously been reserved for the nobility and clergy. Liberty was defined not just as freedom from oppression but as the ability to participate in public life, make choices, and express oneself without interference. This definition of liberty went beyond the personal; it was a societal liberty, asserting that people had the right to shape their government and participate fully in civic life.

The declaration also emphasized **equality before the law**, another groundbreaking concept at the time. The legal system under the Ancien Régime had been riddled with privileges that allowed nobles and clergy to avoid taxes, influence judicial outcomes, and receive preferential treatment. By asserting that all citizens were equal before the law, the declaration demanded that justice apply to everyone, regardless of birth or social class. This was a radical shift from the old order, where the nobility enjoyed exemptions and could influence the legal system to protect their own interests. In the new France, the law would no longer be a tool for the powerful; it would serve the people as a whole.

Individual rights were clearly articulated in the declaration, and they included freedoms that modern societies now consider fundamental. Article 11, for example, protected the freedom of expression, stating that "the free communication of ideas and opinions is one of the most precious of the rights of man." This was a direct response to the censorship that had existed under the monarchy, where dissenting voices were silenced, and publications critical of the government were banned. With this article, the assembly made a powerful statement that a free society must allow its citizens to speak openly, even if their views challenged the government. This freedom of expression was intended to create a society in which ideas could flourish and people could hold their leaders accountable.

The declaration also addressed **property rights**, which were seen as essential to individual freedom and security. Property rights allowed citizens to control their own resources and labor, a stark contrast to the feudal system, where land ownership had been concentrated in the hands of the nobility and clergy. Article 17 declared property to be "an inviolable and sacred right," placing it alongside liberty and security as a core principle. By guaranteeing property rights, the assembly sought to empower individuals and create a society where everyone had the chance to build wealth and security without interference from the state or local lords. Property ownership was not just an economic issue; it was tied to personal autonomy and the right to independence.

One of the declaration's most forward-thinking elements was its commitment to **popular sovereignty**—the idea that legitimate government comes from the will of the people. Article 6 asserted that "law is the expression of the general will," a concept directly drawn from Rousseau. This idea represented a monumental shift in thinking, placing the power to govern in the hands of the citizens rather than a monarch. Popular sovereignty suggested that all public officials, from lawmakers to judges, were accountable to the people and had a duty to serve their interests. It redefined the role of government, making it clear that leaders were not rulers but servants of the public, chosen to protect and promote the collective welfare.

Security was also an essential value in the declaration, as the assembly wanted to ensure that citizens felt protected by the state rather than threatened by it. Article 12 stated that "the protection of the rights of man requires public military forces," recognizing the need for a state that could safeguard individual rights and defend against internal and external threats. However, this security was intended to serve the people, not to enforce the authority of a king or privileged class. The assembly envisioned a system where the government's role in maintaining security was balanced by a respect for individual freedoms, preventing the abuses that had characterized the old regime.

In drafting the Declaration of the Rights of Man and Citizen, the National Assembly sought to **create a document that was both universal and practical**. They wanted principles that could guide the formation of laws, shape the new government, and serve as a permanent reminder of the Revolution's ideals. The declaration was not a legal code, but it was a moral and philosophical foundation for the new France. It outlined what the Revolution stood for and the kind of society its leaders wanted to build—a society where power was derived from the people, laws protected every citizen equally, and personal freedoms were guaranteed. The declaration became a blueprint for a modern state, capturing the aspirations of an era that sought to redefine human rights and inspire future generations around the world.

Influence of Enlightenment Thought

The **Declaration of the Rights of Man and Citizen** drew heavily from the intellectual framework established by Enlightenment thinkers. These philosophers had challenged traditional views of authority, hierarchy, and justice, advocating instead for reason, equality, and individual rights. Their ideas about governance, society, and human nature became the philosophical backbone of the declaration, which sought to apply these principles in real, transformative ways. In drafting the document, members of the National Assembly leaned on Enlightenment concepts to craft a vision for a society where power came from the people, not the crown, and where all individuals had inherent rights that the state was obligated to protect.

Jean-Jacques Rousseau's ideas on popular sovereignty were pivotal in shaping the declaration's stance on government and citizenship. Rousseau had argued in *The Social Contract* that a legitimate government derives its authority from the general will of the people, not from any divine or hereditary right. This concept of popular sovereignty directly influenced Article 6 of the declaration, which states, "Law is the expression of the general will." For the assembly, embracing Rousseau's ideas meant challenging the monarchy and asserting that laws and governance must reflect the people's desires and welfare. Rousseau's emphasis on the "general will" called for a government that was not merely representative but fully accountable to its citizens, serving the common good over any individual or privileged group.

Montesquieu's vision of a balanced government, with separate branches to check each other's powers, also inspired the drafters. Montesquieu's work *The Spirit of the Laws* had argued that dividing power was essential to prevent tyranny. Though the Declaration of the Rights of Man and Citizen did not lay out a government structure in detail, its principles reflected Montesquieu's influence by promoting accountability, transparency, and equality before the law. By endorsing these values, the declaration laid the groundwork for a state that would protect citizens from the unchecked authority that had characterized the Ancien Régime. This dedication to lawful, balanced governance was a stark departure from the absolutism that had previously allowed kings to wield power with little regard for the rights of their subjects.

John Locke's ideas on natural rights were foundational to the declaration's articulation of individual freedoms. Locke had proposed that every person was entitled to life, liberty, and property, rights that he believed governments should protect above all else. The assembly adapted Locke's framework, asserting in Article 2 that the "natural and imprescriptible rights of man" included "liberty, property, security, and resistance to oppression." Locke's belief in the right to property, in particular, resonated with the assembly's aim to create a society where individuals could own and manage their resources without interference from the state or feudal lords. This recognition of property as a natural right gave citizens a sense of autonomy and control over their lives, reinforcing the broader idea that the government existed to serve and protect the people.

The **Enlightenment's emphasis on reason and progress** permeated the declaration, particularly in its commitment to legal and social reform. Philosophers like Voltaire had criticized the arbitrary nature of monarchical rule, where laws were inconsistent and often unfairly enforced. In response, the declaration called for equality before the law, requiring that laws apply to all citizens without exception. By insisting on fair and transparent laws, the declaration echoed Voltaire's vision of a just society founded on reason and justice, one where authority was exercised in service of the public rather than for the benefit of the few.

The influence of **Enlightenment humanism** was evident in the declaration's language, which framed rights as universal and inherent. This idea was radical for a society still emerging from a rigid class structure that viewed social hierarchy as natural. The Enlightenment had argued that human beings shared a fundamental dignity and worth, which the declaration expressed by asserting that "men are born and remain free and equal in rights." This statement didn't just aim to abolish noble privilege; it proclaimed that every individual was entitled to respect and rights by virtue of being human. Enlightenment thought pushed the assembly to see rights as unchangeable, rooted in nature rather than granted by rulers, thus legitimizing the people's demands for political and social equality.

Secularism, another Enlightenment principle, also found its way into the declaration. Enlightenment thinkers like Diderot and Rousseau had questioned the role of organized religion in government, arguing that the Church's influence often worked against individual freedom and scientific progress. While the declaration did not call for a full separation of church and state, it emphasized rights that reduced religious authority's hold over individuals, particularly in matters of conscience and expression. By promoting freedom of thought and speech, the declaration limited the Church's power to dictate beliefs, aligning the revolutionary government with Enlightenment ideals of secular governance and personal freedom.

Key Rights and Freedoms Established

The **Declaration of the Rights of Man and Citizen** established a groundbreaking set of rights and freedoms that defined the aspirations of the French Revolution. By asserting these rights as "natural and imprescriptible," the National Assembly made clear that these were not privileges to be granted or withdrawn by a monarch but fundamental entitlements for every individual. This commitment to universal rights was revolutionary, aiming to reshape French society around values of liberty, equality, and justice.

Liberty was a cornerstone of the declaration, and Article 1 made this plain by stating, "Men are born and remain free and equal in rights." This principle of liberty went beyond freedom from oppression; it included the right to make personal choices, participate in public life, and express oneself without interference. The declaration envisioned a society where citizens could pursue their own paths, unhindered by class restrictions or arbitrary authority. Liberty, as outlined in the declaration, became a defining goal of the Revolution, marking a sharp departure from the controls imposed by the monarchy and the feudal system.

The declaration's commitment to **equality before the law** addressed one of the most oppressive aspects of the Ancien Régime. For centuries, noble birth had meant special treatment, exemption from taxes, and control over the legal system, while the lower classes bore the burdens without recourse. The declaration eliminated these distinctions, insisting that the law must apply equally to all citizens, regardless of social standing. This principle aimed to dismantle a system in which the privileged could manipulate justice to their advantage. Equality before the law promised fairness and consistency, giving the common people a voice and the assurance that the law would protect them as much as it did the powerful.

Freedom of expression was a transformative right included in the declaration. Article 11 recognized the "free communication of ideas and opinions" as a "most precious right." Under the monarchy, censorship had been widespread, and criticism of the government or Church was often punished harshly. By securing freedom of expression, the declaration empowered citizens to speak openly, debate ideas, and hold their leaders accountable. This freedom was not just about speech; it represented a broader commitment to intellectual freedom, encouraging a society where ideas could flourish and individuals could contribute to public discourse without fear.

The right to **security** was also central to the declaration, ensuring that citizens could live without fear of arbitrary arrest or punishment. Article 12 asserted that public forces should exist solely for the protection of citizens' rights, a direct rejection of the monarchy's practice of using military power to enforce its will. Security meant that individuals would be safeguarded by the law, not threatened by it. This protection extended beyond physical safety; it included a guarantee against abuses of authority, reinforcing the idea that the state's duty was to serve its citizens rather than dominate them.

Property rights were similarly enshrined as an essential freedom, affirming that citizens had the right to control and enjoy their possessions. For a country where land and wealth had long been monopolized by the nobility and the Church, this was a radical shift. Article 17 declared property to be "an inviolable and sacred right," giving individuals the assurance that their property was protected by the state. This right supported economic independence, allowing citizens to build wealth and security, free from the exploitation that had defined the feudal system. Property rights gave people a stake in society, connecting personal ownership to political freedom.

The right to **resistance to oppression**, outlined in Article 2, was one of the declaration's boldest statements. This right recognized that people could challenge a government that violated their rights. Resistance to oppression justified the Revolution itself, giving citizens a moral and legal basis for action against unjust rulers. It transformed the role of government from an absolute authority to a contract between the state and the people, where the people held the power to resist if that contract was broken. This right was a call to vigilance, a reminder that government was accountable to its citizens, not the other way around.

Global Influence of the Declaration

The Declaration of the Rights of Man and Citizen had a profound global influence, setting a new standard for human rights and political freedoms. Drafted in 1789 during the early stages of the French Revolution, the declaration laid out principles that resonated far beyond France, inspiring reformers and revolutionaries around the world. Its message was clear: all individuals possessed inherent rights that governments should protect, not restrict. By asserting rights as universal rather than specific to France, the declaration presented an ideal that could apply to any society, regardless of its traditions or political structure. This vision of equality, liberty, and fraternity helped ignite new movements for freedom across the globe, echoing the Enlightenment ideals that had shaped its content.

Europe was the first region where the declaration's influence was keenly felt, particularly in countries under monarchical and aristocratic rule. Reform-minded thinkers in places like Spain, Italy, and the German states closely followed events in France, where the declaration's assertion that "Men are born and remain free and equal in rights" was both radical and compelling. European intellectuals saw in the declaration a blueprint for dismantling feudal privileges and establishing equal treatment under the law. Pamphlets, newspapers, and books translated the declaration's articles into local languages, spreading its ideas to those who sought to challenge authoritarian systems. Political dissidents across Europe drew inspiration from the declaration's principles, fueling calls for representative government, constitutional protections, and individual rights. These ideals eventually contributed to the revolutionary wave that swept through Europe in the early 19th century, as groups sought to emulate the French model of citizen-based governance.

In **Latin America**, the declaration was equally influential, especially among leaders and thinkers who were grappling with the legacy of colonial rule. Inspired by the declaration's bold assertion of universal rights, Latin American revolutionaries saw their struggles for independence from Spain and Portugal as part of a broader fight for justice and autonomy. Figures like **Simón Bolívar** and **José de San Martín** viewed the declaration's emphasis on popular sovereignty as a justification for overthrowing colonial powers and establishing new nations governed by the will of the people. Bolívar, in particular, saw the French Revolution as a powerful example, and his vision for a united, republican South America was deeply influenced by the declaration's ideas. In Mexico, **Miguel Hidalgo's** call for independence also reflected the declaration's values, as he demanded that indigenous and mestizo populations receive the same rights as their European-descended counterparts. The declaration's emphasis on universal rights gave Latin American leaders a framework for building independent states that aimed to uphold justice and equality, even if they faced complex social hierarchies and tensions.

The **United States** found common ground with the declaration as well, particularly since its own Declaration of Independence in 1776 had established similar ideals. Figures like **Thomas Jefferson** and **Benjamin Franklin**, both of whom had been deeply involved in the American Revolution, were influential in shaping French thought during their time in Paris, and they recognized the commonality between the American and French declarations. However, the French declaration went further in its scope, specifying rights not only to liberty and property but also to equality and the resistance to oppression. American abolitionists and suffragists would later point to the French declaration as a model that went beyond the U.S. Constitution's limited view on rights, using it to argue for the universal application of liberties to all people, regardless of race or gender. In this way, the declaration became a tool for expanding the American understanding of rights, showing that freedom and equality were not just goals for nations but for all of humanity.

In **Haiti**, the declaration had perhaps one of its most immediate and transformative impacts. Enslaved and free Black Haitians took the principles of the declaration seriously, interpreting them as promises of freedom and equality that should apply to all people, regardless of race or origin. The most famous figure associated with this movement was **Toussaint Louverture**, who led the Haitian Revolution against French colonial forces. The declaration's assertion that all men were born free and equal directly contradicted the institution of slavery in the French colonies, fueling demands for emancipation among the enslaved population.

When the French government initially refused to extend the declaration's rights to its colonies, Louverture and other revolutionary leaders saw this as hypocrisy and took up arms. The result was the Haitian Revolution, the first successful slave-led revolt in history, which led to the creation of the first Black republic. Haiti's victory sent shockwaves across the Atlantic world, demonstrating the power of the declaration's principles to inspire radical social and political change.

In **Asia**, the declaration influenced reformers who were challenging colonial oppression and autocratic rule. In Japan, where Western ideas were beginning to make an impact during the 19th century, scholars looked to the French declaration as they began pushing for modernization and political reform. Japanese intellectuals and reformists found the declaration's language of human rights and popular sovereignty relevant as they envisioned a new society during the Meiji Restoration. In the **Ottoman Empire**, too, reform-minded officials saw the declaration as a model for modern governance, and they began pushing for the establishment of a constitution and limits on imperial power. The declaration's ideals became a point of reference for those who sought to reform traditional structures and embrace a new, rights-based view of government.

The **global impact of the declaration** wasn't limited to revolutionary movements; it also influenced international discourse on human rights and equality. Philosophers, writers, and politicians cited the declaration when arguing for rights that transcended national borders. For example, in the **19th-century European liberal movements**, advocates called for constitutions and citizens' rights that mirrored the French model. Political activists across the world began to view human rights not as privileges granted by a particular regime but as inherent, universal rights that should be protected regardless of the governing authority. The declaration's language eventually found echoes in the 20th-century United Nations' **Universal Declaration of Human Rights** (UDHR), which was adopted in 1948. When drafting the UDHR, international leaders looked back to the French declaration as one of the earliest comprehensive articulations of universal rights, and many of its principles directly informed the UN's declaration.

The declaration's impact reached **movements for women's rights** as well. Although the document itself focused primarily on men, **Olympe de Gouges**, a French playwright and political activist, published her *Declaration of the Rights of Woman and the Female Citizen* in 1791. She challenged the National Assembly's narrow view on rights, demanding that the ideals of liberty, equality, and fraternity apply to women as well. De Gouges's declaration set an early foundation for the feminist movement, pushing activists in France and beyond to question why rights should be limited by gender. This demand for gender equality continued to influence feminist movements throughout the 19th and 20th centuries, inspiring calls for universal suffrage and equal rights for women around the world.

The **Declaration of the Rights of Man and Citizen** thus served as a powerful template for individuals and movements seeking justice, equality, and freedom. Its ideas transcended borders, taking root in societies both familiar and foreign to the Revolution.

CHAPTER 8: WOMEN IN THE REVOLUTION

Women's March on Versailles

The **Women's March on Versailles** on October 5, 1789, was one of the most remarkable and transformative events of the French Revolution. It began as a response to the severe bread shortages and high prices that had left the people of Paris desperate and starving. For the women of Paris, who were largely responsible for feeding their families, these shortages felt like a direct assault on their ability to survive. Angry, frustrated, and determined to demand action, they gathered at the city's marketplaces and started to talk about their grievances. What began as small discussions soon grew into a massive, organized movement as women called on each other to march to Versailles, the lavish palace where King Louis XVI and Queen Marie Antoinette resided, to confront them directly.

The morning of October 5 saw hundreds, then thousands, of women gathering in the streets. Many of them were working-class market women known as **poissardes**, who were known for their resilience and strength. They wore simple clothes, armed themselves with whatever they could find—pikes, sticks, kitchen knives—and set out on foot. Some women even commandeered cannons. They were joined by men along the way, but this was a **women-led march**, driven by a sense of urgency and a fierce determination to secure bread and make their voices heard. By the time they left Paris, the crowd was nearly 6,000 strong, and as they marched the 12 miles to Versailles in heavy rain, their numbers continued to grow.

The march was driven by **anger at the monarchy's extravagance and detachment** from the suffering of ordinary people. The women knew that Versailles was a world away from the realities of life in Paris, and they were fed up with the king and queen's lavish lifestyle while they struggled to feed their families. Rumors had spread that the king's soldiers had held a feast just days earlier, mocking the new revolutionary tricolor cockades, symbols of the people's struggle. This insult, combined with their desperation for food, added fuel to their anger. Many of the women chanted slogans against the queen, who was often blamed for France's economic problems and accused of spending extravagantly on personal luxuries while the people went hungry.

The marchers arrived at **Versailles by evening**, soaked from the rain but undeterred. They were exhausted, but their purpose was clear: they wanted to speak to the king and demand relief. A delegation of women was allowed inside to meet with Louis XVI, who promised to distribute bread to the people of Paris. However, this promise wasn't enough. The women wanted more than temporary relief; they wanted the royal family to understand their plight. They began to demand that the king return to Paris with them, where he could see the suffering firsthand and be held accountable to the people rather than living in isolation at Versailles.

As the night wore on, tensions escalated. A group of marchers broke into the palace grounds, and a violent confrontation erupted. The palace guards were overwhelmed, and some were killed in the chaos. The women pushed forward, breaking into the queen's chambers, shouting for Marie Antoinette, who narrowly escaped to the king's quarters. The marchers saw this confrontation as necessary to make the monarchy aware of their suffering and frustration. Their direct action showed the king and queen that the people's anger was real and that they were willing to act if their needs continued to be ignored.

By the morning of October 6, the women had achieved their goal: they convinced **Louis XVI to return to Paris** with his family. As the royal procession left Versailles, the women proudly marched alongside the king's carriage, chanting and waving weapons. Some even carried pikes adorned with the heads of the guards they had killed, a shocking and raw display of their anger. The royal family's journey back to Paris was humiliating; they had lost their untouchable status and were now subject to the will of the people. For many Parisians, the king's return to the capital symbolized a shift in power, a sign that the monarchy could no longer ignore or hide from the people's demands.

The **Women's March on Versailles sent a powerful message** across France: ordinary people, especially women, would not be silenced or dismissed. They had made their voices heard at the very heart of royal power, demonstrating that they would not accept empty promises. This march wasn't only about bread; it was a declaration that the people expected meaningful change. The women's march solidified their role in the Revolution, showing that women were essential to the movement and capable of influencing politics and decisions.

This event had **long-lasting effects** on the Revolution. With the king and queen now residing in Paris, they were much closer to the pressures of revolutionary Parisian life and more susceptible to the influence of the National Assembly and the public. The royal family's move from Versailles to the Tuileries Palace marked the beginning of the monarchy's slow decline, as the king and queen lost the symbolic power and distance that Versailles had afforded them. The presence of the monarchy in Paris also created new tensions, as the Assembly, the people, and the king were now closer than ever, both physically and politically.

The march also **inspired other groups to take direct action**. It showed that when people organized and demanded change, they could make things happen, even against the highest authorities. The poissardes and other women who marched that day became symbols of the Revolution's energy and determination. Their actions challenged the notion that politics was a man's domain, showing that women's voices and demands were not only relevant but could be decisive in shaping the course of history. The Women's March on Versailles would be remembered as a defining moment of people-powered change, driven by women who refused to accept a system that left them powerless and hungry.

Role of Women's Societies and Clubs

During the French Revolution, **women's societies and clubs** became vital spaces where women could organize, discuss politics, and advocate for their interests. These groups provided a forum for women to engage actively with revolutionary ideas, often addressing issues that male-led groups overlooked or dismissed. At a time when women had no formal political power, these clubs gave them a platform to push for change, demand rights, and make their voices heard in the midst of a transforming society. The most well-known of these clubs was the **Society of Revolutionary Republican Women**, founded in 1793, which quickly gained attention and influence.

The Society of Revolutionary Republican Women, led by figures like **Claire Lacombe** and **Pauline Léon**, was one of the most outspoken groups advocating for women's rights. They argued that women should have an equal stake in the new political order being forged and demanded that their contributions to the Revolution be recognized. Lacombe and Léon, both passionate and fearless, used the society to push for issues that directly affected working-class women, like fair wages, access to bread, and an end to poverty. The society's meetings were fiery and intense, reflecting the members' deep frustration with being excluded from the very government they had helped bring into existence.

These societies didn't limit themselves to discussions; they took action. Members organized marches, distributed pamphlets, and even confronted political leaders to ensure their voices weren't ignored. Women's societies raised awareness about how economic hardships and food shortages affected women and children, issues they felt the male-dominated National Assembly was not addressing adequately. They demanded that the new government ensure bread and basic necessities for all families, not just the wealthy. In doing so, they connected the ideals of liberty and equality to everyday survival, pushing the Revolution to address the practical needs of the people, especially the poor.

The societies also advocated for **women's right to bear arms and defend the Revolution**. Pauline Léon famously presented a petition to the National Assembly, requesting that women be allowed to form their own militia units. She argued that women were just as capable of defending France from internal and external threats as men were. Although her proposal wasn't accepted, it was a bold statement that women wanted to be active participants in the Revolution, both politically and militarily. By making this demand, women's clubs challenged traditional gender roles and showed that women could be as patriotic and committed to revolutionary ideals as men.

In addition to the Society of Revolutionary Republican Women, other clubs, like the **Fraternal Society of Patriots of Both Sexes**, brought together men and women in a shared space to discuss politics and revolutionary ideas. This club encouraged both sexes to learn about and discuss the political landscape, fostering a sense of camaraderie and mutual respect. The Fraternal Society addressed issues of equality, demanding that women have the same rights and privileges as men within the new republic. Its members viewed the Revolution as an opportunity to rewrite social norms, arguing that liberty and equality meant little if women were still denied a voice in government and society.

The women's clubs became active in **debating laws and policies** that affected women's lives directly. They closely followed the National Assembly's decisions, especially regarding marriage, divorce, inheritance, and property rights. Many women felt that true revolutionary change had to extend beyond the political arena and into family and economic life. They pushed for laws that would give women more control over their own property and access to divorce, viewing these changes as essential for women's independence. The clubs helped politicize these issues, turning them into public debates and pressuring lawmakers to consider the practical implications of equality for women.

Women's societies and clubs often faced **opposition from male leaders**, who were uncomfortable with women's direct involvement in politics. Some male revolutionaries saw the women's clubs as threatening, arguing that women should return to their traditional domestic roles. Over time, hostility toward women's societies grew, and by 1793, the government began to crack down on these clubs, ultimately banning the Society of Revolutionary Republican Women. Despite these restrictions, the clubs had already made a lasting impact by pushing the boundaries of women's participation in the Revolution and forcing political leaders to confront women's issues as part of the revolutionary agenda.

Revolutionary Women Leaders

Throughout the Revolution, a number of **revolutionary women leaders** emerged who dedicated themselves to the ideals of liberty and equality, often at great personal risk. These women were not only advocates for women's rights; they were also influential figures within the broader revolutionary movement. They led marches, organized societies, wrote pamphlets, and engaged directly with political leaders, showing that women were powerful agents of change. Figures like **Olympe de Gouges**, **Claire Lacombe**, and **Pauline Léon** became symbols of female resistance and commitment to revolutionary principles.

Olympe de Gouges was one of the most prominent women of the Revolution, known for her writing and her unyielding advocacy for women's rights. In 1791, she published the *Declaration of the Rights of Woman and the Female Citizen*, a direct response to the Declaration of the Rights of Man and Citizen. In her work, de Gouges argued that the principles of liberty, equality, and fraternity should apply to women as well as men. She called for equal political rights, the right to vote, and the right to participate fully in government. Her declaration was radical and provocative, challenging the male-centered view of citizenship in revolutionary

France. Though her ideas were dismissed by many male revolutionaries, de Gouges's work inspired future generations of feminists and remains a landmark document in the history of women's rights.

Claire Lacombe, an actress turned revolutionary, co-founded the Society of Revolutionary Republican Women and became a vocal advocate for working-class women. Known for her fiery speeches and commitment to radical action, Lacombe believed that the Revolution would be incomplete if it didn't include social and economic equality for women. She often confronted members of the National Assembly, demanding that they take immediate steps to address poverty, food scarcity, and inequality. Lacombe didn't shy away from using strong rhetoric to make her points, and her courage earned her the admiration of many working women who saw her as a champion of their struggles. Lacombe's leadership showed that women could engage in political activism with the same intensity as men, pushing the Revolution to address issues of social justice beyond the typical political debates.

Pauline Léon was another influential figure, known for her commitment to arming women and defending the Revolution. Like Lacombe, Léon co-founded the Society of Revolutionary Republican Women and used her platform to advocate for women's rights. One of her boldest actions was presenting a petition to the National Assembly, demanding that women be allowed to form a militia and participate in the defense of the Revolution. Léon argued that women were capable of defending their homes and communities and should have the opportunity to train with arms. Although her petition was ultimately rejected, Léon's courage and determination to claim a space for women in the Revolution made her an iconic figure among revolutionary women.

Théroigne de Méricourt, another prominent revolutionary, supported women's involvement in political discourse and often attended Assembly meetings dressed in a red liberty cap, a symbol of revolutionary fervor. Méricourt advocated for women's education and saw herself as an intellectual who could bridge the gap between men and women in revolutionary politics. She pushed for women's political inclusion and the right to participate in public debate, often clashing with male leaders who felt that women should not engage in politics. Her presence and activism were symbolic; she represented the courage of women who sought to take part in reshaping France. Méricourt's boldness inspired many women to believe that they, too, could have a role in shaping their nation.

These women leaders were **essential to the Revolution's spirit**, bringing forward issues and perspectives that male leaders overlooked. They challenged gender norms and stood as testaments to women's capacity for leadership, resilience, and courage in the face of social and political obstacles. Their efforts pushed the Revolution to expand its vision of equality, setting a powerful precedent for future generations of women.

Struggles for Rights and Recognition

During the French Revolution, **women faced immense struggles for rights and recognition** in a society that largely viewed politics as a man's domain. Despite their significant contributions to the revolutionary cause—from leading marches to organizing clubs and advocating for reform—women found themselves consistently sidelined in the political process. As the Revolution progressed, they confronted the harsh reality that even radical change might not include them in its vision of equality. The fight for women's rights became both a personal and collective struggle as they battled against entrenched social norms and a political system that resisted giving them an official role.

Women like **Olympe de Gouges** attempted to assert their place in the Revolution by writing and speaking out about the need for gender equality. In her *Declaration of the Rights of Woman and the Female Citizen* (1791), she openly challenged the male-centric Declaration of the Rights of Man and Citizen, arguing that the rights and freedoms being declared as universal should apply equally to women. De Gouges demanded political rights, including the right to vote and participate in governance, as well as social rights like legal equality in marriage and family. Her bold calls for equality, however, were often dismissed by male revolutionaries, who saw her views as disruptive. For de Gouges and her supporters, the refusal to recognize women's rights was a painful reminder of the Revolution's limitations, exposing how deeply ingrained gender discrimination remained even within a movement that claimed to champion equality.

The **Society of Revolutionary Republican Women**, co-founded by Claire Lacombe and Pauline Léon in 1793, became a hub for women to push back against these barriers. Through this society, working-class women voiced their frustrations and organized around issues that directly impacted them, such as the scarcity of food and fair wages. These women argued that, as active participants in the Revolution who had risked their lives in protests and marches, they deserved a say in the political future of France. The society confronted male authorities, demanding recognition of women's efforts and their right to political involvement. However, instead of gaining influence, the Society often encountered hostility. Many male leaders feared that allowing women into the political sphere would destabilize the social order and undermine masculine authority. In response to the Society's growing influence and demands, the revolutionary government eventually banned women's political clubs altogether, silencing one of the few spaces women had created for political expression.

In addition to political exclusion, women faced **constant criticism and accusations of impropriety** when they stepped outside their traditional roles. Revolutionary women who participated in marches or joined societies were often portrayed as unruly or overly emotional, suggesting they lacked the rationality needed for political life. Théroigne de Méricourt, a vocal advocate for women's rights who attended political assemblies and debates, was often mocked for her outspokenness and independent spirit. Her visible involvement in politics led to brutal personal attacks, with critics attempting to discredit her as immoral or unfit for public life. Méricourt's experience illustrated the double standard women faced: while men could engage in passionate revolutionary discourse, women who did the same were stigmatized and ostracized, their reputations tarnished as a warning to others.

The challenges women faced in achieving recognition also extended to the laws and policies passed by the National Assembly, which consistently ignored women's rights. When divorce was legalized in 1792, many women saw it as a victory, as it allowed them to escape abusive or unhappy marriages. However, the law was primarily designed with men's needs in mind, and it did little to improve women's standing in other legal matters, such as inheritance and property rights. Women found that while they could now leave a marriage, they still had limited control over their finances and were often left in poverty. The few legal changes that occurred were insufficient, as they failed to address the underlying inequality women faced in all aspects of life.

The dismissal of women's rights during the Revolution came not only from conservative factions but also from radical leaders who otherwise championed equality. Maximilien Robespierre, a leading figure in the Jacobin movement, believed in the ideals of liberty and justice but argued that women's participation in politics would lead to chaos and moral decay. Robespierre and other male revolutionaries argued that women's primary role was within the home, supporting the family and instilling revolutionary values in their children. This perspective was a severe blow to revolutionary women, who felt betrayed by the very leaders who had inspired them to fight for change. The rejection of their political rights left them disillusioned and aware of the limits of revolutionary rhetoric when it came to gender equality.

Women who dared to challenge these views faced **personal risks and social consequences**. Olympe de Gouges, for example, paid the ultimate price for her activism. As her writings became more outspoken and critical of the government, she was eventually arrested and charged with treason. In 1793, she was executed by guillotine, a stark reminder of the risks revolutionary women faced when they demanded equality. De Gouges's death underscored the dangers of opposing a system that continued to deny women's rights, even as it professed to break from the past. Her execution sent a chilling message to other women, warning them of the potential cost of challenging the Revolution's gendered limits.

The struggles for recognition weren't limited to formal political rights; they also extended to the daily challenges women faced in public life. Revolutionary women were constantly fighting for the right to walk in the streets unharassed, to speak without fear of reprisal, and to demand basic necessities without being dismissed. The Women's March on Versailles had highlighted these issues, showing the power and resolve of women as they demanded bread and attention to their needs. Yet even after this monumental act, women found themselves pushed to the sidelines as male leaders debated their exclusion. The refusal to grant women equal status became a constant battle that forced revolutionary women to assert their place in public life repeatedly, only to encounter ongoing resistance.

Despite these struggles, revolutionary women's actions set a precedent for future movements. By organizing, marching, and demanding their rights, they laid the groundwork for generations of women who would continue to fight for recognition and equality. The Revolution may not have granted women the freedoms they sought, but it exposed the contradictions in a society that preached liberty while denying it to half its population. Women's efforts to claim their rights during the Revolution reflected their resilience and conviction, even in the face of profound resistance. Their struggle for recognition showed that the path to equality would be long and difficult, but it would not be abandoned.

CHAPTER 9: REFORMS AND REORGANIZATION OF FRANCE

Economic and Tax Reforms

The **economic and tax reforms** introduced during the French Revolution transformed France's financial landscape and marked a sharp departure from the system of the Ancien Régime. Under the old regime, France's taxation was deeply unequal. The Third Estate—the common people, who made up the vast majority of the population—shouldered nearly the entire tax burden, while the nobility and clergy enjoyed exemptions and privileges that allowed them to amass wealth without contributing proportionally to the state's revenue. These inequalities fueled resentment, especially as France's financial crisis worsened in the late 1780s. To address these grievances and bring stability to the national economy, the National Assembly introduced sweeping reforms aimed at creating a fair and transparent tax system that would distribute the financial responsibilities of the state more equitably.

One of the most significant steps in tax reform was the **abolition of the feudal system**, which included eliminating many of the dues and payments that peasants had been forced to make to their landlords. These dues, known as feudal obligations, had allowed the nobility to extract wealth from the peasantry through fees on land use, grain mills, and other basic necessities. With the August Decrees of 1789, the National Assembly ended these feudal privileges, effectively freeing peasants from the burdens that had kept them in poverty for centuries. By removing these obligations, the Assembly aimed to give rural communities a chance to improve their economic standing and participate more fully in the new economy. This step also symbolized a broader shift in power, as landowners lost their traditional means of controlling and profiting from peasant labor.

The Assembly also tackled **tax exemptions for the nobility and clergy**, which had long been a point of contention. These two privileged estates, which together made up only about 2% of the population, had enjoyed extensive tax breaks while the Third Estate bore the brunt of public financing. In 1789, the Assembly decreed that tax exemptions based on social class would be abolished, ensuring that all citizens, regardless of status, were subject to the same tax laws. This reform was revolutionary in itself, as it challenged the very foundation of the Ancien Régime's hierarchical society. Now, taxation would be based on income and property rather than birthright, creating a system that was far more equitable and reflective of the revolutionary ideals of equality and fairness.

To streamline tax collection and reduce corruption, the National Assembly introduced a **centralized tax system**. Previously, tax collection had been managed through a complex network of tax farmers, who were private individuals or companies contracted to collect taxes on behalf of the monarchy. These tax farmers often took a cut for themselves and were notorious for abusing their power, inflating fees, and pocketing portions of the revenue. By replacing tax farming with direct government collection, the Assembly aimed to create a more efficient and honest system. This change also brought transparency, as the government could now track revenue without relying on middlemen, reducing opportunities for corruption and increasing public trust in the system.

One of the most important taxes introduced during the Revolution was the **contribution foncière**, a property tax that applied to all landowners, including nobles and clergy. This tax was designed to be progressive, with wealthier landowners paying more based on the value of their property. The contribution foncière ensured that those with more substantial means contributed a fairer share to the state's revenue. It was a critical shift that recognized land as a source of wealth and sought to tax it accordingly. In addition to raising funds for the government, this tax represented a symbolic redistribution of economic responsibility, requiring the wealthy to support the nation just as much as, if not more than, the common people.

Another reform was the **contribution mobilière**, a tax on movable assets, such as business equipment, livestock, and other property that could generate income. This tax targeted merchants and artisans who possessed valuable tools of trade or production resources, ensuring that individuals who profited from commerce and manufacturing contributed to the state. This tax was particularly significant because it acknowledged the emerging economic power of the middle class, many of whom had been gaining wealth through trade and industry. By taxing movable property, the government sought to broaden its tax base and secure contributions from all economic sectors, reinforcing the Revolution's commitment to shared fiscal responsibility.

The National Assembly also introduced a **unified tax on income**, the contribution personnelle et mobilière, which was applied directly to individual earnings. Unlike previous taxes that had targeted consumption or specific goods, this income tax was designed to be comprehensive, encompassing all sources of personal revenue. It provided the government with a reliable source of revenue that grew with the economy, ensuring that as people's earnings increased, so did their contributions to the state. This progressive approach to taxation aligned with revolutionary ideals by attempting to reduce inequality and prevent the excessive accumulation of wealth in a few hands.

In addition to tax reforms, the Assembly sought to stabilize the economy by issuing **assignats**, a form of paper currency backed by confiscated Church lands. These lands, which had been taken over by the state in 1789, were a vast source of potential wealth. The assignats were initially intended as a way to finance the government and pay off France's mounting debt, but they quickly became a primary currency in circulation. This approach had mixed results; while it provided immediate financial relief and allowed the government to avoid excessive borrowing, the assignats soon became overissued, leading to inflation and devaluation. However, the use of assignats illustrated the Assembly's willingness to experiment with new economic policies to stabilize the country and address its debts.

The state's **seizure of Church lands** also contributed to economic reform. By nationalizing these lands, the government both gained valuable assets and addressed the Church's economic power, which had often functioned as a barrier to equality. Church lands were redistributed or sold to citizens, particularly to peasants who had never owned land before. This redistribution aimed to reduce poverty in rural areas and create a class of independent landowners who would support the Revolution and the new republic. The economic impact of these land sales was significant, as it gave more people a stake in the new government and redefined wealth distribution in a country long dominated by privileged landowners.

The economic and tax reforms of the Revolution were **instrumental in redefining citizenship**. No longer was citizenship based simply on birth or privilege; it now required participation in the state's financial responsibilities. The new tax system reinforced the idea that all citizens, from the wealthiest landowners to the poorest laborers, had a role in supporting the government. This principle helped to foster a sense of national solidarity, as taxation was now tied to the values of equality and shared responsibility. While these reforms met with resistance from some sectors, especially from former nobles and clergy who saw their privileges disappear, they were foundational in shaping a more modern and democratic France.

Church and State Separation (Civil Constitution of the Clergy)

One of the most transformative reforms during the French Revolution was the **Civil Constitution of the Clergy**, a 1790 law that sought to restructure the Church's role in French society and fundamentally redefine the relationship between Church and state. The Catholic Church had held vast wealth and power in France for centuries, with its influence reaching deep into the political and social realms. It owned significant land, collected tithes from the people, and maintained a close alliance with the monarchy. This privileged position allowed the Church to function almost as a parallel government, often unaccountable to the state and isolated from the needs of the general population. The National Assembly saw this setup as incompatible with the revolutionary ideals of equality and accountability and aimed to bring the Church under state control to reduce its power and redistribute its wealth.

The **Civil Constitution of the Clergy** effectively placed the Church under the authority of the state. Priests and bishops would no longer answer solely to the Pope but would instead be elected by local communities, with the state overseeing these elections. This was a radical change; by democratizing the Church hierarchy, the Assembly intended to make the clergy more responsive to the needs of their congregations rather than to distant authorities in Rome. To many revolutionaries, this reform was essential to creating a truly representative government. If priests were elected like other public officials, they would, in theory, serve the interests of their communities and uphold revolutionary values rather than acting as mere agents of the Vatican.

This restructuring included a major financial shift as well. The Assembly **abolished the tithe**, the traditional tax that parishioners had been obligated to pay to the Church. Tithes had long been a source of resentment, especially among peasants who could barely afford to pay for their basic needs. By removing this tax, the government lifted a financial burden from the poor and redirected the Church's income stream to the state. In exchange, the state promised to provide salaries for priests and bishops, effectively making them civil servants. This was a profound change in the Church's role: clergy would now be financially dependent on the state, reinforcing the idea that they were accountable to the new government rather than a separate ecclesiastical hierarchy.

The decision to **nationalize Church property** was also part of the Civil Constitution's sweeping changes. The Assembly seized Church lands, which constituted nearly 10% of all land in France, and sold them to raise funds for the state. These lands were valuable assets, and their sale helped stabilize the French economy, allowing the state to fund its operations without relying solely on increased taxation or borrowing. This land redistribution also allowed many ordinary citizens, particularly members of the middle class and wealthier peasants, to purchase property, which had previously been out of reach. The redistribution of Church lands not only brought in much-needed revenue but also symbolized the transfer of power from the old feudal and ecclesiastical elites to the people.

However, the Civil Constitution of the Clergy sparked **deep divisions within French society**. For devout Catholics, the state's intervention in Church matters was an attack on their faith. Many priests and bishops resisted the Civil Constitution, refusing to take an oath of loyalty to the state as it required. This refusal created two distinct groups within the French clergy: the "constitutional" priests, who swore allegiance to the state, and the "non-juring" or "refractory" priests, who remained loyal to the Pope and the traditional Church hierarchy. This split deepened the rift between revolutionaries and religious conservatives, as many parishioners sided with refractory priests and viewed the state's actions as a betrayal of Catholicism.

The revolutionary government's attempt to bring the Church under its control led to **religious and regional tensions**. In regions like the Vendée and Brittany, where Catholicism was deeply ingrained in local identity, resentment toward the Civil Constitution grew. People felt that the state was attempting to undermine their faith, leading to significant resistance. These areas became centers of counter-revolutionary activity, with uprisings fueled by anger over the perceived assault on religious freedom. The state's efforts to enforce the Civil Constitution of the Clergy often led to violent confrontations, escalating tensions and contributing to a civil war that would continue to challenge revolutionary authority.

Despite the controversies, the Civil Constitution of the Clergy was seen by many revolutionaries as a **necessary step toward modernizing France**. They believed that separating the Church from its vast political and economic power would help eliminate one of the key pillars of the old feudal system. By reducing the Church's authority and financial independence, the Assembly hoped to create a secular state where loyalty was directed toward the nation rather than religious institutions. This secular vision aligned with Enlightenment ideals that called for reason and science to govern public life, free from the influence of religious dogma. For the Assembly, the Church's alignment with the monarchy and its resistance to reform made it an obstacle to true liberty and equality.

The Civil Constitution also inspired discussions on **freedom of religion**. By controlling the Church's role in state matters, the Assembly sought to ensure that no religious institution could hold power over the people's political rights. Although this didn't guarantee complete religious freedom, it was a step toward a secular state where people's rights were not dictated by religious affiliation. The reforms set a precedent for later laws that would further separate Church and state, laying the groundwork for modern secularism in France.

Administrative and Legal Changes

In addition to religious reforms, the Revolution brought sweeping **administrative and legal changes** that restructured the very fabric of French governance. The National Assembly aimed to streamline France's complex and often inefficient administrative divisions, which had been a source of confusion and corruption under the Ancien Régime. One of the most significant changes was the creation of **departments**, a new administrative system that divided France into 83 equal units. These departments replaced the old provinces and were designed to eliminate the influence of local aristocrats and ensure that all regions adhered to the same laws and regulations. Each department had its own elected officials and councils, making governance more localized but also more standardized across the country.

The Assembly also implemented the **Napoleonic Code**, a unified legal code that replaced the patchwork of laws that had previously governed different regions. This code enshrined principles of equality before the law, property rights, and individual liberties, standardizing laws across France and ensuring that citizens were subject to the same legal protections and obligations. By creating a single legal framework, the Napoleonic Code aimed to remove privileges based on birth and ensure that everyone, regardless of social status, had the same rights.

The judiciary underwent substantial changes as well. The Assembly established **public courts** with elected judges to replace the seigneurial courts controlled by local lords, eliminating the influence of the nobility in legal matters. This shift allowed for a fairer judicial process, where justice was less likely to be manipulated by powerful families.

CHAPTER 10: THE RISE OF FACTIONS AND POLITICAL CLUBS

Emergence of the Jacobins, Girondins, and Others

As the French Revolution deepened, political clubs and factions emerged, each with distinct ideologies and visions for France's future. These groups provided a platform for debate, strategy, and mobilization, becoming key forces in shaping the Revolution. Among the most influential were the **Jacobins** and the **Girondins**, who would come to represent two different approaches to revolutionary goals and governance. These clubs, along with others that rose and fell during the Revolution, illustrated the political diversity and tensions that marked the revolutionary period.

The **Jacobins** were initially a group of moderate reformers when they formed in 1789, meeting in a former convent in Paris. The club began as a space for deputies to gather and discuss revolutionary ideas outside the formal structures of the National Assembly. Named after their meeting place, the Jacobins' full title was the "Society of the Friends of the Constitution." However, as the Revolution progressed, the Jacobins grew increasingly radical, aligning themselves with the interests of the urban poor, or sans-culottes, and advocating for more direct democracy. They attracted members like **Maximilien Robespierre**, whose dedication to revolutionary ideals and uncompromising vision for a republic of virtue made him one of the most influential figures within the club. By 1792, the Jacobins were the Revolution's leading voice for radical reform, demanding the overthrow of the monarchy and advocating for strict measures against counter-revolutionaries.

Robespierre's vision and leadership transformed the Jacobins into an instrument for **political purges** and centralized control. Under his influence, the Jacobins pushed for the Reign of Terror, believing that harsh measures were necessary to defend the Revolution from internal and external threats. They supported the idea of a revolutionary government that had the authority to suspend individual liberties temporarily to preserve the Revolution's principles. This stance alienated many moderate supporters, but it strengthened the Jacobins' influence over Paris and helped them gain control over the revolutionary government. The Jacobins became synonymous with the most radical phase of the Revolution, advocating for a France that would be free from monarchy, privilege, and counter-revolutionary forces.

In contrast, the **Girondins** represented a more moderate approach to the Revolution. Originating from the Gironde region in southwestern France, this faction was composed mainly of provincial leaders, intellectuals, and merchants who were initially aligned with the Jacobins. The Girondins shared the Jacobins' desire to see an end to the monarchy, but they envisioned a more decentralized government and believed in protecting individual freedoms even during revolutionary times. Leaders like **Jacques-Pierre Brissot** and **Jean-Marie Roland** argued that the Revolution needed to balance revolutionary fervor with caution, warning against the dangers of mob rule and the concentration of power in Paris. The Girondins feared that the Jacobins' radicalism would lead to despotism, and they advocated for a more controlled and balanced approach that protected civil liberties.

The **Girondins and Jacobins increasingly clashed** over their vision for France's future. Girondins believed in engaging with other European nations diplomatically and argued for a system that would allow individual provinces more autonomy rather than concentrating power in Paris. They favored a representative democracy that respected local governance and opposed the Jacobins' centralizing tendencies. This division became especially pronounced when it came to the issue of war. The Girondins, including Brissot, supported a military campaign against Austria and Prussia, believing that spreading revolutionary ideals across Europe would help secure the Revolution at home. The Jacobins, initially cautious about foreign war, feared that it might strengthen the monarchy's power, but as the conflict escalated, they came to support it as a means to defend the Revolution.

These ideological divisions **intensified political rivalry** between the two factions, with each side accusing the other of betraying revolutionary principles. As the Revolution's crises grew, the Jacobins saw the Girondins as counter-revolutionaries who were obstructing progress and protecting the interests of the bourgeoisie over those of the people. The Girondins, in turn, saw the Jacobins' reliance on the sans-culottes and their increasingly violent tactics as a path to tyranny. This rift came to a head in 1793 when, after a series of political maneuvers and accusations, the Jacobins succeeded in purging the Girondins from the National Convention. Many leading Girondins were arrested, tried, and eventually executed, effectively consolidating the Jacobins' control over the revolutionary government.

Beyond the Jacobins and Girondins, other **political clubs and factions** emerged, reflecting the diversity of thought and interests within the Revolution. The **Cordeliers Club**, founded by figures like **Georges Danton** and **Camille Desmoulins**, was notable for its populist stance and its support for direct action. The Cordeliers were among the earliest advocates for insurrection, arguing that the people had a right to take up arms to defend their freedoms. Unlike the Jacobins, who leaned toward centralized government, the Cordeliers emphasized the need for broad political participation and direct democracy, where ordinary citizens could hold leaders accountable through public action. The Cordeliers were influential in mobilizing the sans-culottes and were instrumental in the popular uprisings that shaped the Revolution's most radical phases.

Meanwhile, the **Feuillants** represented the conservative end of the revolutionary spectrum. Formed by moderate constitutional monarchists in 1791, the Feuillants broke away from the Jacobins when it became clear that the latter were pushing for a republic. The Feuillants believed in a constitutional monarchy, similar to Britain's model, where the king's power would be limited by law, but he would still serve as the head of state. They saw the monarchy as a stabilizing force and believed that radical republicanism would lead to chaos. However, as the Revolution's radicalism intensified, the Feuillants found themselves increasingly isolated and ultimately irrelevant as their vision of a constitutional monarchy was rejected by the revolutionary momentum that favored a republic.

The political clubs of the Revolution weren't confined to the elites; they had **branches and networks** that reached into the working-class neighborhoods of Paris and beyond. Clubs in smaller cities and towns allowed ordinary citizens to engage with revolutionary politics, discuss issues, and participate in decision-making. These clubs became centers of political life, where people debated not only national policies but also local concerns and community welfare. They provided a space for the exchange of ideas, a platform for marginalized voices, and an avenue for citizens to feel a direct connection to the revolutionary government. The clubs distributed pamphlets, organized rallies, and encouraged civic participation, shaping public opinion and driving revolutionary fervor from the ground up.

The competition among these factions and clubs created a **vibrant but volatile political culture** in revolutionary France. As each group sought to advance its vision, alliances formed and dissolved, creating a landscape of shifting loyalties and fierce ideological battles. The struggle between the Jacobins and Girondins highlighted how quickly unity could unravel as political stakes rose. For all the factions involved, the Revolution was a living, breathing process—something that could be influenced, shaped, and steered in different directions. This dynamic brought energy to the Revolution but also created instability, as factional rivalries led to internal conflicts that would shape the course of French history.

By 1794, as the Reign of Terror peaked, the Jacobins under Robespierre had solidified their dominance, and **political opposition was suppressed** with brutal efficiency. Yet, the suppression of the Girondins, Cordeliers, and other political groups ultimately narrowed the diversity of voices in the Revolution. As dissent was stifled, the Jacobins' unchecked authority became a source of fear and resentment, even among former supporters. By the time of Robespierre's fall, many revolutionaries had grown wary of any faction's total control. The Revolution's later stages would see a backlash against this radical dominance, as factions and clubs were gradually silenced or absorbed into the government, ending a period of intense political diversity that had defined the Revolution's early years.

The emergence of factions like the Jacobins, Girondins, Cordeliers, and Feuillants demonstrated the power of ideas to drive political change and set a precedent for organized political engagement that would influence France—and later revolutions—around the world.

Debates on Governance and Policies

The **debates on governance and policies** during the French Revolution were intense and complex, reflecting the diverse ideologies and ambitions of the different factions. At the heart of these debates were questions about the nature of the new French government, the role of the monarchy, the extent of individual freedoms, and the definition of "equality." Each faction had its own vision for how to structure France's future, and as the Revolution progressed, these debates grew more polarized, revealing deep divisions over how to interpret revolutionary ideals.

For the **Jacobins**, the Revolution's goal was a radical transformation of French society and governance. The Jacobins, led by figures like Robespierre and Saint-Just, argued that a truly revolutionary government should reflect the general will and prioritize the common good over individual interests. They believed in a **centralized government** that could enforce unity and prevent counter-revolutionary influence. To the Jacobins, individual freedoms could be temporarily restricted if doing so safeguarded the Revolution's ideals. This approach led them to support policies that restricted the press, suspended civil liberties, and allowed the Committee of Public Safety to operate with considerable authority. They saw these measures as necessary to root out enemies of the Revolution and secure the new republic.

On the other hand, the **Girondins** advocated for a more decentralized approach to governance. Coming primarily from provincial regions, the Girondins believed that the Revolution should empower local communities and give citizens control over their affairs without excessive interference from Paris. They argued that the Jacobins' centralization was authoritarian and warned that concentrating power in the capital would alienate the provinces. In debates, the Girondins often called for **representative democracy** and respect for individual freedoms, pushing back against policies they viewed as tyrannical. They argued that the Revolution's success depended on balance—a government that could maintain order without resorting to the drastic measures that the Jacobins endorsed. This belief led them to oppose the Reign of Terror, warning that indiscriminate purges and repression would ultimately harm the Revolution's moral foundation.

The question of **monarchy** was another contentious issue. Early in the Revolution, many factions believed that a constitutional monarchy could balance revolutionary goals with political stability. The Feuillants, a conservative faction, strongly advocated for this model, believing that the king could serve as a unifying figurehead while the Assembly handled governance. The Jacobins, however, grew increasingly opposed to any form of monarchy. Robespierre and other radicals saw the monarchy as incompatible with the principles of liberty and equality, arguing that Louis XVI's actions had demonstrated his opposition to revolutionary ideals. For the Jacobins, executing the king was a necessary act to dismantle the old regime fully. The Girondins, while critical of the monarchy, were hesitant about execution, fearing that such an action would radicalize the Revolution beyond repair.

Economic policies were a particularly divisive issue, especially regarding how to manage food shortages and inflation. The Jacobins, aligning themselves with the urban poor, advocated for price controls on essential goods, particularly bread, to ensure that all citizens could afford basic necessities. Robespierre saw economic equality as essential to true liberty, arguing that without access to food and resources, people could not be genuinely free. The Girondins, however, feared that strict economic regulation would harm merchants and stifle commerce. They argued for a **free market** approach, warning that government intervention would discourage trade and create a dependency on the state. This division underscored their differing priorities: while the Jacobins focused on economic equality as part of social justice, the Girondins prioritized economic freedom and feared that overregulation would lead to authoritarianism.

Foreign policy also spurred fierce debate among the factions. The Girondins, particularly figures like **Brissot**, believed in a revolutionary war to spread France's ideals across Europe. They saw foreign monarchies as threats to the Revolution and argued that a proactive approach would both secure France and inspire other nations to rise against their own oppressive governments. The Jacobins were initially cautious about foreign intervention, fearing that war would strengthen the monarchy and put the Revolution at risk. However, as conflict became inevitable, the Jacobins embraced the war as a tool for defending the Revolution, especially as foreign armies advanced toward French borders. The war debates highlighted the factions' differing views on France's role in Europe—whether it should spread its ideals actively or focus on securing its own stability first.

The **use of violence and the concept of justice** became a dividing line between factions. The Jacobins, particularly during the Reign of Terror, believed that justice required rooting out anyone who might endanger the Revolution, even if it meant executing perceived counter-revolutionaries. Robespierre saw terror as an unfortunate but necessary method for defending the people's rights against enemies who would dismantle the Revolution. The Girondins condemned this approach, viewing mass arrests and executions as abuses of power. They argued that a revolution founded on liberty and justice could not be sustained by fear and oppression. For the Girondins, the Jacobins' use of terror was a betrayal of the Revolution's ideals, and they fought to limit the Committee of Public Safety's power.

These intense debates over governance and policies **reflected deeper philosophical differences**. The Jacobins were willing to sacrifice certain freedoms temporarily to ensure the Revolution's survival and ultimate success, while the Girondins believed that revolutionary ideals should guide every decision. The competing visions made consensus nearly impossible, driving a wedge between the factions and ultimately leading to the Girondins' expulsion and persecution during the Reign of Terror. The Jacobins' dominance after this period marked the height of radical revolutionary policies, pushing the Revolution in an increasingly authoritarian direction even as it claimed to serve the people's interests.

The Role of Public Opinion and Political Clubs

Public opinion and political clubs became powerful forces during the French Revolution, shaping the direction of policies and amplifying the voice of ordinary citizens in unprecedented ways. Political clubs like the **Jacobins**, **Cordeliers**, and **Girondins** acted as centers of discussion, debate, and action, influencing public opinion and the government's decisions. These clubs gave citizens a place to engage with revolutionary ideas, bringing politics into the public sphere where ideas could be openly discussed and shared. For the first time, people who had previously been excluded from politics—artisans, shopkeepers, and laborers—were able to participate, shaping a new political culture that valued civic engagement.

The Jacobin Club was especially effective in mobilizing **public opinion**. Its members understood the importance of reaching a broad audience and used pamphlets, speeches, and newspapers to communicate their ideas. Jacobin leaders like Robespierre and Danton spoke directly to the concerns of the sans-culottes, the working-class people who struggled with high bread prices and economic hardship. The Jacobins' alignment with the sans-culottes gave them considerable influence in Paris, where public opinion was critical to the Revolution's direction. Through their speeches and publications, the Jacobins framed the Revolution as a fight for the common people, contrasting themselves with factions they accused of betraying the Revolution's ideals. This populist approach helped the Jacobins solidify their power and maintain public support during times of crisis.

The **Cordeliers Club** was another influential group, known for its radical stance on direct democracy and the rights of the people. The Cordeliers emphasized the people's right to hold their leaders accountable, advocating for frequent assemblies and the right to protest and petition. Figures like **Desmoulins** and **Danton** used the Cordeliers Club to call for direct action, urging Parisians to demand justice and fair treatment from their government. The Cordeliers' approach resonated with the sans-culottes, who saw the club as a champion of their interests. The club's meetings attracted large crowds, and their calls for action often led to protests or demonstrations, which pressured the government to address pressing issues like food shortages and inequality. Through the Cordeliers, ordinary citizens found a platform that prioritized their needs, bringing their voices directly into revolutionary politics.

Political clubs also became **centers of propaganda and public discourse**, influencing how people viewed the Revolution's events and leaders. Each faction used publications, pamphlets, and newspapers to shape public opinion, often engaging in fierce battles of rhetoric. The Girondins published articles critical of the Jacobins' authoritarian tendencies, warning that Parisian dominance threatened the provinces' autonomy. The Jacobins, in turn, painted the Girondins as elitists who ignored the needs of the poor and protected counter-revolutionaries. This rivalry was not limited to political debates within the Assembly; it spilled into the streets, where citizens engaged in these discussions and took sides. Public opinion became a battleground where factions sought to win popular support, demonstrating that the Revolution was not just fought in the halls of government but also in the minds of the people.

In addition to shaping public discourse, **political clubs facilitated civic participation**, turning spectators of the Revolution into active participants. Clubs encouraged members to discuss policies, draft petitions, and attend public demonstrations, often giving them a say in issues that affected their communities. This level of involvement fostered a sense of ownership over the Revolution, as people began to see themselves as stakeholders in France's political future. Public opinion, shaped by these discussions, became a powerful tactic that could push the government to act. When the people felt that their leaders were straying from revolutionary ideals, they had the means to make their dissatisfaction known through clubs and the protests they organized. This bottom-up pressure kept revolutionary leaders aware that their power depended on the people's approval.

The spread of clubs beyond Paris also demonstrated the **influence of public opinion in the provinces**. Clubs in cities like Lyon, Marseille, and Bordeaux brought revolutionary ideas to regions that might otherwise have felt disconnected from the events in the capital. Local clubs allowed citizens in these areas to engage with and influence the national discourse, ensuring that revolutionary ideas spread and took root across France. In provincial cities, clubs provided a critical link between Paris and local communities, fostering a national network of revolutionary ideals and public involvement. These clubs ensured that debates over policies, governance, and justice were not confined to elites but included voices from all regions. By encouraging civic engagement and amplifying public opinion, the political clubs made the Revolution a truly collective endeavor. This widespread participation in political life redefined what it meant to be a citizen in revolutionary France, embedding public opinion as a powerful force that influenced government decisions and shaped the Revolution's course.

CHAPTER 11: WAR WITH NEIGHBORING MONARCHIES

Causes of the Revolutionary Wars

The **causes of the Revolutionary Wars** that erupted in 1792 were rooted in a complex mix of political, ideological, and diplomatic factors. As the French Revolution intensified, it sent shockwaves across Europe, challenging not only France's internal structure but also the stability of monarchies and established powers across the continent. The revolutionary ideas of liberty, equality, and the dismantling of feudal privilege threatened the traditional order that many European monarchs relied upon to maintain control. Neighboring monarchies, such as Austria and Prussia, viewed the revolutionary developments in France with a mix of fear and anger, concerned that France's upheaval might inspire similar rebellions within their own borders. The Revolution quickly became a European concern, setting the stage for conflict.

One of the primary **catalysts for the Revolutionary Wars** was the increasing tension between France and Austria, where Queen Marie Antoinette's family, the Habsburgs, ruled. The French monarchy had traditionally maintained a close alliance with Austria, cemented by the marriage of Marie Antoinette and Louis XVI. However, as the Revolution progressed, these ties were severed, and many revolutionaries viewed Austria as a hostile power, particularly due to Marie Antoinette's position as queen. To the revolutionaries, Austria symbolized the oppression and privilege they sought to overthrow. They suspected that Marie Antoinette maintained secret communications with her family, raising fears of a potential Austrian intervention to restore the French monarchy and protect her interests. The animosity toward Austria fed the perception that foreign powers posed a direct threat to the Revolution.

Ideological fervor was also a driving factor behind the push for war. Many revolutionaries believed that the ideals of the Revolution—liberty, equality, and fraternity—should not be confined to France alone but should inspire similar transformations throughout Europe. Figures like Jacques-Pierre Brissot, a prominent member of the Girondins, argued passionately for a "crusade for liberty," envisioning a war that would liberate other European peoples from monarchical oppression. Brissot and his supporters believed that revolutionary France had a duty to spread its principles beyond its borders, not only to protect its own Revolution but also to encourage a Europe-wide revolt against tyranny. They saw war as a moral imperative, a means to extend the revolutionary ideals and to challenge the old order wherever it stood.

The **internal divisions within France** further heightened the call for war. By 1792, the Revolution was deeply polarized, with factions like the Girondins and Jacobins vying for influence. The Girondins, who favored aggressive foreign policy, saw war as a way to unify the French people and silence domestic opposition by rallying the nation around a common cause. They argued that victory on the battlefield would legitimize the Revolution and demonstrate France's strength to its enemies, both foreign and internal. The Jacobins, particularly Robespierre, were initially skeptical of war, fearing that it would strengthen the monarchy and the aristocracy by giving them control over military affairs. However, as the situation escalated, even the Jacobins came to accept that war might be inevitable to defend the Revolution from a hostile Europe.

In addition to these ideological and political motivations, **diplomatic missteps and provocations** contributed significantly to the onset of war. In August 1791, Emperor Leopold II of Austria and King Frederick William II of Prussia issued the **Declaration of Pillnitz**, which stated that they would intervene in France if the Revolution endangered the monarchy. Although this declaration was meant to be a warning rather than a direct threat, many in France perceived it as an act of aggression. Revolutionaries saw the Declaration of Pillnitz as evidence that foreign monarchs would not hesitate to intervene to crush the Revolution, reinforcing the view that France needed to act preemptively to protect its gains. The declaration amplified fears of an international conspiracy against France, and revolutionaries believed that war was the only way to confront this looming threat.

The actions of émigrés—nobles and supporters of the old regime who had fled France—also had a role in increasing tensions. Many émigrés settled in Austria and other neighboring countries, where they lobbied European monarchs to take action against revolutionary France. They exaggerated the violence and disorder within France, hoping to persuade foreign powers that intervention was necessary to restore stability. The presence of émigré armies, which gathered on France's borders with the intention of launching counter-revolutionary attacks, added to the fear that the Revolution was under siege. Their efforts were a constant reminder to revolutionaries that elements of the old order were actively working to dismantle their achievements, encouraging calls for preemptive action against France's neighbors.

As war became more likely, **economic factors also entered the equation**. France was struggling with severe financial instability, partially due to the debts it had inherited from the monarchy and the costs of the Revolution itself. Many revolutionaries believed that a successful war could lead to the seizure of resources and territories, which would alleviate the financial strain. The idea of conquering new lands and tapping into the wealth of other nations appealed to those who saw France's weakened economy as an existential threat to the Revolution. War was seen as a way to gain resources while also securing the Revolution from the constant threat of royalist and foreign interference.

By the spring of 1792, France's **revolutionary government** had reached a point of no return. The National Assembly, pressured by Girondins and other pro-war factions, declared war on Austria on April 20, 1792. This decision was driven by the combination of ideological zeal, fear of foreign invasion, and the belief that France's survival depended on asserting itself militarily. The war was intended not only to protect France but to establish it as a revolutionary power capable of challenging and, if necessary, overthrowing monarchies across Europe.

Once war was declared, **events quickly spiraled**, drawing other European nations into the conflict. Austria and Prussia allied against France, and soon other monarchies joined the coalition, each fearing the spread of revolutionary fervor. For the revolutionaries, the struggle became an existential fight for the Revolution itself. They saw each new alliance as confirmation that France stood alone against a Europe committed to the old order. To the French people, the war was both a threat and a rallying cry, an opportunity to defend the ideals they had fought so hard to establish.

The Revolutionary Wars escalated rapidly, transforming the Revolution into a **militarized and highly nationalistic movement**. The initial hope of spreading revolutionary ideals through a "crusade for liberty" was soon overshadowed by the need to protect France from foreign invasion. The war intensified internal divisions and gave rise to the Reign of Terror, as revolutionary leaders believed that only strict measures could prevent sabotage from within and invasion from without. For many French citizens, the war became a matter of survival, uniting the population in a shared sense of duty and resistance, even as it exacerbated the Revolution's most radical impulses.

These wars fundamentally altered the Revolution, leading to the rise of military leaders like **Napoleon Bonaparte** who would later capitalize on the nationalistic fervor and military prowess developed during these conflicts.

Early Battles and Mobilization

When France declared war on Austria in April 1792, it faced the immediate challenge of mobilizing an army capable of defending the Revolution against well-trained foreign forces. The French military, weakened by years of internal discord and purges of royalist officers, was not fully prepared for the war. Many experienced officers had fled the country or were dismissed due to their loyalty to the monarchy, leaving gaps in leadership. Revolutionary fervor, however, spurred the government to act quickly. Determined to defend France and spread revolutionary ideals, the leaders of the new republic set about rapidly building an army that could withstand the looming threats from Austria, Prussia, and other European powers.

In the early days of mobilization, enthusiasm ran high. The government called for volunteers, and thousands of citizens responded, driven by a mix of patriotism and revolutionary spirit. The **Levée en masse**, a mass conscription order later introduced in 1793, brought together men from all walks of life, turning the war effort into a national cause. The sense of unity in these early days was strong, and the recruits saw themselves as defenders of liberty, equality, and fraternity. They were not only fighting a traditional military campaign; they were fighting to protect the values of the Revolution from enemies who represented the old order. This motivation gave them a resilience and determination that compensated, in part, for their lack of formal military training.

The **first major confrontation** came with the Battle of Valmy on September 20, 1792. This battle was a turning point, marking the first significant victory for the French revolutionary forces against the Prussian and Austrian coalition. Led by General Dumouriez and General Kellermann, the French army, despite being less experienced and organized, managed to repel the coalition forces. The victory at Valmy boosted French morale immensely and gave credence to the idea that the Revolution could defend itself against foreign powers. It also fueled the belief that ordinary citizens, fighting for a cause they believed in, could stand up to professional armies. Valmy became a symbol of the strength of the French people united by revolutionary ideals, inspiring further mobilization and strengthening the resolve of those back home.

After Valmy, the French revolutionary government took further steps to expand the army and mobilize resources. The government issued **calls for more conscripts**, creating an army that grew rapidly in size. Reforms within the military sought to promote officers based on merit rather than birth, a revolutionary idea that reflected the values of equality and capability over aristocratic privilege. This reorganization allowed talented soldiers from humble backgrounds to rise through the ranks, creating a more motivated and cohesive fighting force. The new structure helped the French military become more flexible, adaptable, and driven by ideological commitment rather than traditional hierarchy. For many soldiers, serving in the revolutionary army was an honor and a duty, a way to protect the Republic they believed in.

The early battles also revealed the **brutal realities of revolutionary warfare**. Fighting alongside regular troops were the sans-culottes, radical citizens who volunteered for the front lines, bringing with them a fierce loyalty to the revolutionary cause. Many of these fighters lacked proper training and equipment, and the army often struggled with logistics and supply issues. Food shortages, insufficient arms, and harsh conditions created immense challenges, testing the endurance of the troops. Yet the sense of collective purpose and the fear of foreign subjugation kept morale high, and the victories achieved in these early engagements only strengthened their resolve. France's ability to mobilize effectively against better-prepared armies was a testament to the power of revolutionary zeal.

Internal Opposition and Foreign Threats

As France entered into war with neighboring monarchies, it faced not only external enemies but also a wave of **internal opposition** that threatened to destabilize the revolution from within. Various factions within France held differing opinions on the Revolution, and the start of the war intensified these divisions. Monarchists and royalists, still loyal to the crown and the old order, opposed the Revolution's radical changes and saw the war as an opportunity to restore the monarchy. Many of these counter-revolutionaries supported the coalition forces, hoping that a foreign intervention would defeat the revolutionary government and bring stability to France. They openly challenged revolutionary leaders, sometimes even sabotaging war efforts by disrupting supply lines and spreading misinformation.

The revolutionary government responded with suspicion and a firm resolve to root out internal threats. Fearing that royalists and counter-revolutionaries could undermine the Revolution from within, they implemented policies to identify and suppress internal dissent. This led to the formation of the **Committee of Public Safety** and the surveillance of suspected counter-revolutionaries, particularly in areas known for their royalist sympathies, such as the Vendée. The Vendée region, where deep religious and royalist loyalties ran strong, became a hotbed of counter-revolutionary activity. Armed uprisings broke out as locals resisted conscription and rejected the Revolutionary government's policies. The insurrection in the Vendée led to a brutal internal conflict, forcing the revolutionary army to divert resources from the foreign front to suppress rebellion at home.

This **internal opposition** exacerbated the challenges of the foreign threat, especially as news of uprisings and betrayal spread throughout France. Revolutionary leaders began to view any form of dissent as a potential act of treason, leading to widespread arrests and the purges of suspected counter-revolutionaries. The government's concerns weren't unfounded; many émigrés— French nobles who had fled during the Revolution—were actively lobbying foreign monarchs to support a military intervention that would restore the old regime. These émigrés formed alliances with foreign powers and spread exaggerated accounts of revolutionary chaos, painting the Revolution as a violent rebellion that required European intervention to restore order. Their influence made the coalition's goal not only to halt the Revolution's spread but to reinstate the monarchy in France.

In response to these **growing internal and external threats**, the revolutionary government adopted more radical measures. The Committee of Public Safety gained sweeping powers to monitor and control the population, aiming to ensure loyalty to the revolutionary cause. This period saw the intensification of the Reign of Terror, as leaders like Robespierre argued that strict measures were necessary to protect the Revolution from internal and foreign enemies. Revolutionary tribunals were set up to try and execute those accused of counter-revolutionary activities, creating an atmosphere of fear and suspicion. Thousands of citizens, including former nobles, clergy, and political moderates, were arrested or executed. For the revolutionary government, this crackdown was justified as an essential step in safeguarding the Republic. However, for many, it marked a descent into authoritarian rule, blurring the line between defending the Revolution and undermining its ideals.

Meanwhile, **foreign threats grew** as Austria, Prussia, and eventually Britain and other European monarchies formed coalitions to stop the Revolution. These powers viewed the spread of revolutionary ideas as a direct threat to their own stability. The French Revolution challenged the entire European monarchical system, and rulers feared that if revolutionary France succeeded, similar uprisings would follow in their own countries. This collective fear united them in a coalition determined to halt France's revolutionary momentum. As a result, France found itself in a prolonged, multi-front war against some of the most powerful armies in Europe. Each coalition member brought its resources, troops, and military experience to the battlefield, aiming to quash the Revolution and restore monarchical authority in France.

The pressures of war intensified the revolutionary government's drive to **mobilize all available resources**. The Levée en masse, a decree of mass conscription, was introduced in 1793, calling on every citizen to contribute to the war effort. This decree transformed the entire nation into a war machine, mobilizing not only soldiers but also civilians who worked in arms manufacturing, logistics, and support. Every aspect of French society was directed toward defending the Revolution from external invasion and internal insurrection. The idea that all citizens had a role in protecting the Republic became a rallying cry, turning the war into a national struggle for survival.

As the conflict dragged on, the revolutionary army began to gain ground, and **leaders like Napoleon Bonaparte emerged** as effective military strategists, boosting French morale and repelling coalition forces. The successes of these early campaigns demonstrated that France could hold its own against formidable enemies, fueling national pride and reinforcing the idea that the Revolution could survive even against overwhelming odds.

CHAPTER 12: THE REIGN OF TERROR

Rise of the Committee of Public Safety

The **rise of the Committee of Public Safety** in 1793 marked a critical shift in the direction of the French Revolution. At this time, France faced threats on multiple fronts: foreign invasions from a coalition of European monarchies, counter-revolutionary uprisings within its borders, and a collapsing economy that left the public discontented and restless. The revolutionary government believed that drastic measures were needed to protect the gains of the Revolution from both internal and external enemies. As a response to these pressing dangers, the National Convention created the Committee of Public Safety, a small but powerful body intended to provide leadership and stability during this tumultuous period.

Initially, the **Committee of Public Safety** was not meant to be a permanent institution. Established in April 1793, it was intended as a temporary solution to help the National Convention navigate the immediate crisis. The Convention granted the Committee extensive powers to coordinate the war effort, manage economic policy, and maintain public order. It began with nine members and later expanded to twelve, all of whom were drawn from the most committed revolutionary ranks. These men were given the authority to make decisions without the usual checks and balances, operating independently of the Convention's daily oversight. The Committee's rapid decision-making capacity was seen as essential for handling the Revolution's many emergencies.

As the Committee evolved, it became dominated by **Maximilien Robespierre**, one of the Revolution's most ardent defenders. Robespierre, a lawyer by training, held strong ideals about virtue, equality, and the moral purity of the Republic. To him, the Revolution was not merely a political change but a moral crusade that demanded absolute commitment. Under his leadership, the Committee's mission took on a new intensity. Robespierre argued that the Revolution could not be truly safe until all threats—both internal and external—were eliminated. He viewed any opposition as dangerous, interpreting dissent not as a difference of opinion but as a betrayal of the Republic's ideals. This absolutist stance shaped the Committee's policies and set the stage for the **Reign of Terror**.

The Committee's expanded power was a response to a complex and dangerous situation. Foreign armies from Austria, Prussia, Britain, and other monarchies were advancing on France's borders, determined to crush the Revolution before its ideas could spread to their own territories. Internally, regions like the Vendée and cities like Lyon and Marseille erupted in counter-revolutionary revolts, spurred by anger over conscription and radical social changes imposed by the government. To the Committee, these uprisings were existential threats. They believed that allowing rebellion to flourish would undermine the Revolution and potentially open the door for the monarchy's return. The Committee thus saw it as their duty to take drastic action to protect the Republic and its revolutionary ideals.

The **power of the Committee of Public Safety** grew rapidly, particularly as it took control of the war effort. The Committee implemented the Levée en masse, a nationwide conscription policy that mobilized all able-bodied men for military service. This mobilization helped France push back the invading forces and marked a shift toward a total war effort. The Levée en masse also unified citizens under a common purpose, transforming the war from a professional conflict into a mass mobilization of the people. The Committee coordinated supplies, arms production, and logistics, establishing a centralized control that allowed France to field one of the largest armies in Europe. The effectiveness of the Levée en masse gave the Committee further confidence in its approach and reinforced its authority.

In addition to its military initiatives, the Committee of Public Safety enforced **economic controls** to address the severe inflation and food shortages that plagued the country. They implemented the **Law of the Maximum**, a policy that set price caps on essential goods, including bread and flour, to make them more affordable for the poor. The Committee viewed this policy as essential for maintaining popular support, as hunger and scarcity were potent catalysts for discontent. However, enforcing these economic measures proved challenging, leading the Committee to impose strict penalties on anyone caught hoarding or violating price controls. The Committee's interventions in the economy were unprecedented, showcasing their willingness to intervene in all areas of public life to secure the Revolution's stability.

The **Committee's role in enforcing revolutionary justice** was another defining feature of its reign. Believing that France was rife with "enemies of the Revolution," the Committee established revolutionary tribunals to root out counter-revolutionaries, traitors, and anyone perceived as a threat. These tribunals operated with extraordinary speed, often bypassing standard legal protections to deliver swift judgments. Robespierre and his allies on the Committee argued that justice had to be ruthless to deter enemies from undermining the Revolution. The infamous **Law of 22 Prairial**, passed in 1794, further intensified the Committee's judicial reach by allowing the revolutionary tribunals to convict suspects without requiring witnesses or evidence, relying instead on "moral proof." This law made it easier to sentence individuals to death, contributing to the high number of executions during the Reign of Terror.

The Committee's pursuit of "enemies" extended beyond actual counter-revolutionaries to include anyone perceived as insufficiently loyal to the revolutionary government. This environment of **fear and suspicion** permeated French society. Citizens were encouraged to report suspicious behavior, and accusations could be based on mere rumor. This atmosphere turned neighbors against each other, as fear of being accused led many to denounce others to protect themselves. Revolutionary ideals of fraternity and solidarity were increasingly overshadowed by paranoia, as loyalty to the Committee became a matter of survival. This policy of surveillance and suspicion created a chilling effect, silencing dissent and ensuring compliance with the Committee's vision for the Republic.

The Committee's influence peaked in 1794, with **Robespierre's vision of a "Republic of Virtue"** driving its policies. Robespierre believed that France needed to embody the highest moral standards to secure the Revolution's goals. To him, virtue was the foundation of a stable republic, and he saw the Committee's actions as a way to cleanse society of corruption, selfishness, and counter-revolutionary thought. Festivals celebrating revolutionary virtues replaced traditional religious ceremonies, and the Cult of the Supreme Being, a state-sponsored deist religion, was introduced as an attempt to unite the people under a new moral framework. The Committee's campaigns aimed to shape the citizenry's beliefs and behaviors, aligning public and private life with revolutionary principles.

However, the **concentration of power in the Committee** and its increasingly authoritarian policies began to create unease even among revolutionaries. Many leaders who had once supported the Committee's measures grew wary of its unyielding approach and the dominance of Robespierre's vision. The rapid increase in arrests and executions, along with the harsh economic controls, led to growing resentment. The fear that anyone could be accused of counter-revolutionary activities, combined with the Committee's unchecked authority, made many believe that the Revolution was veering into tyranny. Even some of Robespierre's former allies came to see the Committee's actions as a betrayal of the Revolution's original promises of liberty and justice.

The **rise of the Committee of Public Safety** transformed the French Revolution, shifting it into a period defined by stringent control, surveillance, and terror. The Committee's actions, driven by a belief in the need for radical measures to protect the Republic, created a state apparatus that touched every part of life. The push to safeguard the Revolution at all costs reshaped French society, as loyalty to the Committee became synonymous with loyalty to France itself. The Committee's rise highlighted the dangers of unchecked authority and the difficulties of balancing revolutionary ideals with the demands of governance, leaving a legacy that would reverberate far beyond the Revolution's end.

Role of Robespierre and Radical Leadership

During the **Reign of Terror**, Maximilien Robespierre emerged as the Revolution's defining figure, embodying the fervent, uncompromising spirit of the radical leadership that directed this intense phase. Robespierre, often called the "Incorruptible" due to his dedication to revolutionary ideals, believed the Revolution required complete devotion and a willingness to make harsh sacrifices for the sake of the new Republic. To him, the Revolution was not merely a political shift but a moral transformation, one that demanded purity of purpose, unyielding commitment to equality, and the removal of all who threatened these principles. This philosophy shaped the actions he pursued within the Committee of Public Safety, where he wielded significant influence and authority.

Robespierre's radical approach to leadership was deeply influenced by his conviction that **virtue was the foundation of a just society**. Drawing from Rousseau's concept of the "general will," Robespierre envisioned a Republic that reflected the people's best interests, unclouded by personal ambition or self-interest. To him, any deviation from the Revolutionary path was an act of betrayal, and he came to believe that virtue could not coexist with tolerance for dissent. He argued that, to achieve true equality and liberty, France had to rid itself of corruption, selfishness, and counter-revolutionary sentiment. This perspective set the stage for the policies of the Reign of Terror, where loyalty to the Revolution became an unyielding standard enforced by the Committee of Public Safety.

As a leader, Robespierre demanded **absolute loyalty** from both his colleagues and the people of France. He positioned himself as the moral center of the Revolution, holding those around him to a high standard that often led to internal conflict and purges within the government. Robespierre and his allies, particularly Saint-Just, viewed anyone who expressed doubts about their policies or who suggested moderation as potential enemies. Even former allies were not immune to Robespierre's suspicions; figures like Danton and Desmoulins, once close associates, found themselves accused of betraying the Republic when they advocated for easing the harsh measures of the Terror. For Robespierre, friendship and past loyalty were secondary to the Revolution's needs, and he showed little hesitation in condemning those he believed had wavered in their dedication.

Robespierre's vision for the Revolution extended beyond political loyalty to a **moral and social transformation**. He promoted the idea of a "Republic of Virtue," where citizens would embody revolutionary values in every aspect of their lives. His vision was as much about reshaping individual behavior and beliefs as it was about changing laws. To achieve this, he encouraged the promotion of secular festivals, like the **Festival of the Supreme Being**, which celebrated ideals of civic duty, equality, and virtue. Robespierre hoped to replace traditional religious structures with a form of state-sponsored deism, emphasizing reason and moral integrity over dogma. The Cult of the Supreme Being was his attempt to provide the French people with a unifying ethical framework that would replace Catholicism, aligning religious sentiments with revolutionary ideology. However, this effort was controversial and alienated many, even those within his circle, as it highlighted Robespierre's tendency to impose his beliefs on others.

In practice, Robespierre's leadership style created an **atmosphere of intense surveillance and suspicion**. He encouraged citizens to report any signs of counter-revolutionary activity, creating a culture of fear and mistrust. Public support for the Revolution was not enough; people had to demonstrate an active commitment to its ideals. His speeches frequently emphasized the necessity of rooting out corruption and betrayal, reinforcing the belief that enemies of the Revolution lurked everywhere. Under his influence, the Committee of Public Safety adopted increasingly extreme policies, justifying executions as necessary for the Republic's survival. This mindset transformed the Revolution's ideals into a relentless, unforgiving process, where allegiance was measured by complete conformity to Robespierre's vision of virtue.

Despite his idealism, Robespierre's authority was not absolute. He faced **internal resistance** from other factions within the revolutionary government who questioned his methods. The Hébertists, led by Jacques Hébert, advocated for even more radical policies, including the complete dechristianization of France. While Robespierre shared some anticlerical sentiments, he opposed the Hébertists' extreme stance, arguing that it would alienate the population. After deeming the Hébertists' influence too disruptive, Robespierre and the Committee orchestrated their purge, executing Hébert and his supporters in 1794. This action demonstrated Robespierre's ability to eliminate rivals and solidify his control, but it also increased his reputation for intolerance and willingness to turn on former allies.

Robespierre's grip on power became increasingly fragile as his **paranoia deepened**. He came to believe that the Revolution's enemies were everywhere, even within the National Convention and the Committee itself. The Law of 22 Prairial, which expanded the powers of the revolutionary tribunals and stripped accused counter-revolutionaries of the right to a defense, reflected his heightened mistrust. This law allowed the Committee to expedite executions, increasing the number of people condemned to the guillotine. The law's passage marked a peak in the Terror, as the judicial system became little more than a tool for removing anyone perceived as a threat. Under Robespierre's leadership, justice was redefined as loyalty to the Revolution, with death as the penalty for dissent.

Policies of Terror and Purges

The **policies of terror and purges** implemented during the Reign of Terror were rooted in the belief that the survival of the Revolution depended on the complete elimination of its enemies. The Committee of Public Safety, led by Robespierre, wielded its power to enforce conformity, using fear and punishment as tools to suppress any opposition. This approach reshaped the justice system, as revolutionary tribunals replaced traditional courts, empowered to pass sentences quickly and decisively. The tribunals operated under the assumption that anyone could be a counter-revolutionary, creating an atmosphere where guilt was presumed rather than proven. The policies that emerged from this approach blurred the lines between justice and persecution, turning the ideals of liberty and equality into instruments of repression.

The **Law of Suspects**, passed in September 1793, allowed the revolutionary government to arrest individuals on vague grounds, often without concrete evidence. Anyone who was suspected of counter-revolutionary sympathies, had connections to former aristocrats, or even showed insufficient enthusiasm for the Revolution could be detained. This law led to the incarceration of thousands, filling prisons across France and creating a climate of fear. Family members, neighbors, and colleagues became wary of each other, as even casual remarks or previous associations could result in an accusation. The Law of Suspects granted the

Committee of Public Safety sweeping powers to detain people indefinitely, expanding the scope of those considered dangerous to the Republic.

The **Law of 22 Prairial** took these measures further, simplifying the process of convicting and executing suspects. Passed in June 1794, this law allowed revolutionary tribunals to condemn people without the right to a defense or witness testimony. The law defined counter-revolutionary activity in broad terms, encompassing anyone deemed hostile to the Revolution's ideals. Under this policy, public trials became swift judgments, often ending in immediate execution. The removal of legal protections made it nearly impossible for the accused to defend themselves, transforming the tribunals into instruments of terror rather than justice. The law reflected Robespierre's belief that the purity of the Revolution demanded swift, uncompromising action against enemies, real or imagined.

This **escalation of terror extended to all levels of society**. Nobles, clergy, former royalists, and even former revolutionaries were not immune from suspicion. Initially, the Terror targeted aristocrats and known counter-revolutionaries, but it soon widened to include anyone whose loyalty was uncertain. The purges reached into the revolutionary government itself, as figures like Danton and Desmoulins were accused of undermining the Revolution and sent to the guillotine. Danton's execution shocked many, as he had been instrumental in the Revolution's early stages. His fall illustrated the Committee's insistence on ideological purity, revealing that even prominent revolutionaries could become enemies of the state if they strayed from the Committee's vision.

Beyond political opponents, the policies of terror targeted **ordinary citizens** who failed to meet the Committee's expectations of revolutionary conduct. Actions like hoarding food, speaking against price controls, or simply showing apathy toward revolutionary festivals could lead to suspicion. This extended the reach of the Terror into daily life, as citizens became hyper-aware of their behavior to avoid attracting attention. People were expected to display unwavering enthusiasm for the Revolution; anything less risked accusations of counter-revolutionary sympathies. This omnipresent fear forced conformity, as survival often depended on outwardly demonstrating loyalty and dedication to the revolutionary cause.

The **economic policies enforced by the Committee** were also part of the purges, as hoarders and profiteers were singled out and punished. The Law of the Maximum, which set price controls on essential goods, was meant to ensure fair distribution and prevent inflation, but it placed severe restrictions on commerce. Those accused of hoarding or selling goods above the regulated prices faced swift punishment. These economic purges were framed as moral actions, casting hoarders as enemies of the people who exploited others' suffering. The Committee used public trials to make examples of these individuals, sending the message that economic crimes were as punishable as political dissent.

The revolutionary **festivals and ceremonies** introduced by Robespierre and the Committee became tools for reinforcing loyalty, but they also served as litmus tests for citizens' commitment. Events like the Festival of the Supreme Being were designed to unite the population under a shared revolutionary culture, replacing religious traditions with civic rituals. However, these festivals became tests of faith, with those showing insufficient enthusiasm risking suspicion. By turning public ceremonies into displays of loyalty, the Committee of Public Safety used festivals not just to celebrate revolutionary ideals but to gauge the public's allegiance. Attendance was monitored, and enthusiasm was expected; any perceived lack of commitment could raise suspicion. These civic rituals blurred the line between personal belief and state loyalty, forcing citizens to conform outwardly to revolutionary values.

The policies of terror and purges also extended to **regional uprisings**, particularly in places like the Vendée, where royalist and religious loyalties remained strong. The Committee's response to these uprisings was severe, employing military force to crush dissent and executing perceived rebels in mass numbers. The brutal suppression of these regions illustrated the extent of the Committee's commitment to silencing any challenge to the Republic, reinforcing their authority through fear.

Ultimately, the policies of terror under Robespierre's radical leadership drove the Revolution to a breaking point. The Committee's expansive definition of "enemy" turned the Revolution against its own, creating a climate where even the most ardent revolutionaries feared for their lives. By mid-1794, Robespierre's insistence on purity and total commitment alienated many in the government, leading to his eventual downfall. The Reign of Terror ended as Robespierre and his closest allies faced execution, a consequence of the very policies they had enacted. The period left a legacy of caution, as France grappled with the balance between revolutionary ideals and the dangers of unchecked power.

CHAPTER 13: THE FALL OF ROBESPIERRE AND END OF TERROR

Growing Opposition to Robespierre

As the Reign of Terror wore on, **opposition to Maximilien Robespierre began to grow from multiple directions**. His policies and methods, while initially tolerated as necessary for protecting the Revolution, began to alienate both his allies and the wider public. The intense atmosphere of fear, suspicion, and strict control enforced by the Committee of Public Safety began to test the patience and endurance of many revolutionaries. By 1794, Robespierre's image as the uncompromising leader dedicated to virtue and purity transformed into that of a leader who demanded complete obedience, making him an increasingly isolated and controversial figure.

One of the main sources of opposition came from **within the revolutionary government itself**, where members of the National Convention and the Committee of Public Safety grew wary of Robespierre's absolutism. His allies in the Committee, like Saint-Just and Couthon, supported him, but many others felt he was concentrating too much power. The **Law of 22 Prairial**, which simplified the process of convicting and executing those accused of counter-revolutionary actions, shocked even some of his closest associates. The law removed fundamental legal rights, allowing people to be convicted on flimsy evidence or mere suspicion. This approach was seen as excessive and, more importantly, dangerous to anyone in the government, who could be accused and sentenced on the thinnest of pretexts.

Robespierre's **moral rigidity** also alienated those who felt he was pushing his vision of a "Republic of Virtue" too far. His devotion to enforcing revolutionary purity extended beyond politics into the private lives of citizens, demanding adherence to values that some saw as restrictive. The **Cult of the Supreme Being**, which he introduced as a new civic religion, was met with mixed reactions. Many Catholics viewed it as an attempt to replace their faith, while atheists and dechristianizers found it hypocritical and unnecessary. Robespierre's insistence on moral oversight over religion caused resentment among those who valued the Revolution's promises of freedom, making his rule seem overbearing and dogmatic.

Robespierre's **increasing suspicion of allies** also contributed to his isolation. Figures like Georges Danton and Camille Desmoulins, once close friends, had been executed under Robespierre's direction, sending a chilling message to other revolutionaries. Danton's death, in particular, shook many in the National Convention, as he had been a prominent leader and a symbol of the early Revolution. With Danton gone, many felt that no one was safe, and the line between ally and enemy seemed to blur further with each purge. Robespierre's refusal to tolerate any challenge to his authority made him appear paranoid and dictatorial, and his tendency to accuse other revolutionaries of corruption or counter-revolutionary sympathies fueled distrust among those around him.

In addition to internal dissent, **public discontent surged** as Robespierre's policies impacted daily life. The Law of the Maximum, which imposed price controls on essentials, aimed to make goods accessible to the poor but often led to shortages and frustration among merchants. Economic hardships, including rampant inflation, made life difficult for ordinary citizens, who began to resent the Terror's impact on their ability to meet basic needs. For many, the constant fear of arrest and execution was unbearable. The climate of distrust extended into neighborhoods and families, as citizens were encouraged to denounce each other for even minor deviations from revolutionary norms. People feared that a careless comment, a display of insufficient enthusiasm, or an accidental association could lead to imprisonment or death.

Robespierre's **speeches in the National Convention** began to reflect his increasing paranoia and sense of betrayal. He frequently spoke about enemies lurking within the Republic, warning of conspiracies and corruption in every corner. In his infamous speech on **8 Thermidor** (July 26, 1794), he claimed to possess a list of traitors within the Convention but refused to name them. This threat alarmed his fellow deputies, who feared they could be next. Instead of rallying support, Robespierre's vague accusations created a coalition of former allies and political rivals determined to protect themselves from his wrath. By leaving the threat ambiguous, Robespierre inadvertently unified a group of deputies who saw his downfall as the only way to end the escalating terror.

The **Committee of Public Safety itself** began to fracture under the weight of Robespierre's influence. Members who had once worked alongside him now questioned his judgment, concerned that the Committee had become a tool for his personal vendettas rather than a means of protecting the Republic. Figures like Collot d'Herbois and Billaud-Varenne, previously supportive of the Committee's radical measures, turned against Robespierre as his authority grew unchecked. The once-united Committee split into factions, with some members fearful of Robespierre's power and others uncertain of their own safety. This internal division weakened the Committee's overall effectiveness and undermined its claim to be the voice of revolutionary France.

The **sans-culottes**, the working-class citizens who had been strong supporters of the Jacobins and Robespierre, also grew disillusioned as the Terror continued. Initially, they had seen the purges and executions as necessary for defending the Revolution from aristocrats and royalists, but as more common people found themselves caught in the web of suspicion, the sans-culottes began to feel betrayed. They had hoped for a Republic that would improve their lives, yet they now faced the same fear and scarcity as under the monarchy. Their support waned as the executions seemed less about justice and more about silencing any form of dissent, alienating the very people who had once fueled the Revolution's most radical moments.

In the end, Robespierre's **inability to adapt** contributed significantly to the growing opposition. His rigid commitment to revolutionary purity, while inspiring to some, was inflexible and left no room for negotiation or compromise. His unwillingness to consider moderation or alternative perspectives alienated potential allies, who might otherwise have supported him. He refused to see that the Revolution's goals could be pursued without resorting to constant purges and terror. This uncompromising stance, coupled with his growing isolation and paranoia, left him vulnerable to opposition, as he no longer had the support he needed to withstand a challenge.

The **day after his Thermidor speech**, on July 27, 1794, the National Convention turned against him. Members of the Convention, fearful for their lives and increasingly disillusioned with the course of the Revolution, voted to arrest Robespierre and his close allies. In a swift and decisive move, the deputies who once feared him now celebrated his downfall, seeing it as a necessary step to end the Reign of Terror.

Key Events Leading to His Arrest

In the final days before **Robespierre's arrest**, tensions reached a breaking point within the National Convention and the Committee of Public Safety. His speech on **8 Thermidor (July 26, 1794)** was one of the decisive moments that turned his allies against him. In that speech, Robespierre claimed to have knowledge of conspirators within the Convention itself, suggesting that traitors were lurking among the very deputies tasked with upholding the Revolution. However, he refused to name specific individuals, fueling widespread fear and paranoia among the deputies, who worried they might be on his mysterious "list" of traitors. By leaving his accusations vague, Robespierre inadvertently created an atmosphere of alarm and insecurity that united many against him.

On the morning of **9 Thermidor (July 27)**, the tension broke into open opposition. Several deputies, led by figures like **Jean-Lambert Tallien** and **Billaud-Varenne**, took the floor in the Convention, openly denouncing Robespierre as a tyrant. Tallien, carrying a dagger he claimed was to defend himself if Robespierre attempted to harm him, was among the first to speak out, accusing Robespierre of seeking to establish a dictatorship. This display of resistance emboldened others, and one by one, deputies condemned Robespierre and his associates, including **Saint-Just** and **Couthon**. The Convention, once cowed by his authority, began to applaud his accusers, marking a dramatic shift in momentum.

As the Convention's opposition intensified, Robespierre attempted to speak in his defense. Yet, **calls to silence him** drowned out his efforts, and he found himself isolated in the very chamber where he had once held great power. The Convention swiftly voted to arrest Robespierre, along with his closest allies, Saint-Just, Couthon, and Robespierre's younger brother, **Augustin**. Their arrest signaled a dramatic turn in the Revolution, as the Convention moved quickly to end the influence of the radical faction that Robespierre had dominated.

Following their arrest, Robespierre and his allies were taken to the **Hôtel de Ville** in Paris, where supporters attempted a failed last-minute rescue. By the early hours of **10 Thermidor (July 28)**, Robespierre and his companions were captured once again. Later that day, Robespierre, along with 21 of his associates, was guillotined, marking the end of his reign. His fall occurred rapidly and publicly, signaling an end to his policies of terror and purges.

Impact of the Fall and End of Terror

The fall of Robespierre and the end of the **Reign of Terror** dramatically altered the course of the French Revolution. His execution signified the collapse of the radical phase of the Revolution, as the policies of terror and extreme purges that had characterized his leadership came to an abrupt halt. In the immediate aftermath, the National Convention moved swiftly to dismantle the apparatus of terror, dissolving revolutionary tribunals and dismantling the **Committee of Public Safety's** extraordinary powers. This shift represented a deliberate attempt to distance the government from the period of radicalism, and the leaders of the Convention aimed to restore a sense of stability and order.

The end of the Terror marked the beginning of the **Thermidorian Reaction**, a phase in which the government sought to reverse many of the most extreme policies of the previous years. The Convention repealed laws that had enabled mass arrests and executions, including the notorious **Law of 22 Prairial**. These repeals were a crucial step in restoring judicial process and curtailing the power of the tribunals, which had operated with minimal oversight. The release of thousands of political prisoners followed, as the state acknowledged the abuses that had occurred under the guise of revolutionary justice. The government recognized that continuing Robespierre's policies risked alienating the public and intensifying resentment against the Revolution.

With the collapse of Robespierre's leadership, the **political culture** of the Revolution shifted significantly. The intense surveillance and suspicion that had pervaded society began to diminish, as people no longer feared being accused of counter-revolutionary sympathies for minor actions or associations. Many citizens who had lived in constant fear of denunciation and execution found a sense of relief, though the scars of the Terror remained. Neighborhood watch groups, which had been instrumental in reporting suspected counter-revolutionaries, lost their influence, and the atmosphere of mutual distrust began to dissipate. This change allowed a more moderate, less punitive approach to governance to emerge, as the new leaders sought to avoid the authoritarianism that had characterized Robespierre's rule.

Economically, the end of the Terror had a profound impact on France. The **Law of the Maximum**, which had imposed strict price controls on essential goods, was repealed, as the government shifted toward a more laissez-faire approach to the economy. This change brought immediate challenges, as the removal of price controls led to rapid inflation and food shortages that disproportionately affected the poor. Despite these hardships, the repeal of strict economic regulations signaled a broader commitment to restoring individual freedom and market stability. The new leadership hoped that by stepping back from economic intervention, France could recover from the chaos and shortages that had plagued it during the Terror.

Politically, the fall of Robespierre created an opening for **more moderate factions** to reassert control. The Thermidorian leaders, recognizing the public's exhaustion with radicalism, promoted a government based on stability and pragmatism. The **Girondins**, many of whom had been purged or executed during the Terror, were partially rehabilitated, as the government tried to signal a shift away from extreme policies. The leadership also aimed to restore the balance of power, emphasizing legislative authority over the unchecked dominance of a single committee or faction. This realignment was crucial for stabilizing the government, which now sought to regain the trust of a populace wary of autocratic power.

Culturally, the end of the Terror allowed for a **revival of personal freedoms** that had been suppressed under Robespierre's rule. People could once again gather without fear of surveillance, speak freely, and participate in cultural activities that had been curtailed. The public expressed relief at the return of some semblance of normalcy, though the memory of the Terror left a lasting impression on French society. Art, literature, and social life began to flourish again, albeit cautiously, as people tested the limits of the new, less repressive environment. This period also saw a resurgence of religious practices, as the harsh restrictions on worship imposed during the de-Christianization efforts were relaxed.

The end of the Terror had **lasting implications for future French governance**. The Thermidorian Reaction revealed a deep-seated aversion to centralized, unchecked power and reinforced the importance of legal safeguards and protections against tyranny. The leaders of the Convention understood that the Terror had turned many citizens against the Revolution, as the promise of liberty and equality had been overshadowed by repression and fear. Determined to prevent a repeat of these abuses, they began drafting a new constitution that would limit the power of the executive and enshrine the protection of individual rights.

As a result, the **Directory** government that eventually emerged represented a more conservative phase of the Revolution, balancing republican ideals with a pragmatic approach that aimed to restore stability.

CHAPTER 14: THE THERMIDORIAN REACTION AND DIRECTORY ERA

Reforms and Reaction Against Extremism

Following Robespierre's fall in July 1794, the **Thermidorian Reaction** began as a direct response to the extremism that had defined the Reign of Terror. The leaders who emerged after Robespierre's execution sought to dismantle the machinery of terror, restore civil liberties, and curb the radicalism that had pushed France into a cycle of suspicion, purges, and executions. These **reforms against extremism** aimed to stabilize the country, recalibrate revolutionary ideals, and reassure a public exhausted by years of intense political and social upheaval.

One of the first steps taken during the Thermidorian Reaction was the **dismantling of the Committee of Public Safety's power**. While it continued to exist, its authority was significantly reduced, ending its unchecked influence over France's political and judicial systems. This move reflected a commitment to reining in centralized power and restoring the legislative authority of the National Convention, which had been overshadowed by the Committee's dominance. The Convention reduced the Committee's capacity to enforce arbitrary arrests and executions, eliminating the legal mechanisms that had enabled mass purges. By stripping the Committee of its draconian powers, the Thermidorians hoped to restore a balance of power and prevent the rise of future autocratic control.

Revolutionary tribunals were also restructured and gradually phased out. Under Robespierre, these tribunals had operated with extraordinary speed and often bypassed standard judicial procedures, resulting in thousands of executions based on suspicion alone. The Thermidorians repealed the **Law of 22 Prairial**, which had simplified the process of condemning people to death, giving tribunals the authority to sentence individuals without a proper defense or witnesses. With the repeal, the judicial system returned to a semblance of normalcy, where accusations were scrutinized more carefully, and legal protections were reinstated. This reform marked a major step in returning France to the ideals of justice and liberty that had initially inspired the Revolution.

To further distance the government from the oppressive measures of the Terror, the Thermidorians **freed political prisoners** who had been incarcerated under accusations of counter-revolutionary activity. Thousands were released, and those who had lost property or status under the Committee's decrees were allowed to return home. The release of these prisoners was both a symbolic and practical move, illustrating the Thermidorians' commitment to reversing Robespierre's policies of suspicion and punishment. It sent a message to the public that the era of arbitrary arrests and ideological purges was over, restoring a sense of security and stability for citizens who had lived in constant fear of denunciation.

In addition to judicial reforms, the Thermidorians **lifted the economic controls** that had been put in place to manage food shortages and stabilize the economy. During the Terror, the Committee had imposed the **Law of the Maximum**, which controlled the prices of essential goods to make them affordable to the public. While intended to ease the economic strain on the lower classes, these controls often led to black markets, shortages, and resentment among merchants and farmers. By removing price controls, the Thermidorians sought to revive the economy and encourage free-market practices. However, this policy shift led to rapid inflation, and food prices soared, sparking discontent among the urban poor who struggled to afford basic necessities. Despite these challenges, the Thermidorians remained committed to liberal economic reforms, hoping that a freer market would eventually bring stability.

The **role of religion** also underwent significant changes during the Thermidorian Reaction. The dechristianization efforts of the radical phase had led to the closure of churches, persecution of clergy, and the introduction of revolutionary festivals intended to replace religious practices. Many people, especially in rural areas, had deeply resented these policies, viewing them as an assault on their faith and traditions. Recognizing the need to ease these tensions, the Thermidorians allowed churches to reopen and permitted public worship, though the government remained officially secular. The policy shift allowed citizens to practice their religion without fear of repression, helping to reduce rural unrest and resentment toward the Revolution.

As part of their efforts to curb extremism, the Thermidorians targeted the **Jacobins**, who had been the main architects of the Terror. The once-powerful Jacobin Club, which had dominated Parisian politics and mobilized public opinion in favor of radical measures, was shut down. Many prominent Jacobins were arrested or forced into exile, and local Jacobin clubs across France were disbanded. This move was both symbolic and practical, as the Thermidorians sought to purge the government of the factions that had enabled Robespierre's dominance. The closure of the Jacobin Club signaled a clear rejection of the radicalism that had characterized the Revolution's recent past, marking a shift toward a more moderate, controlled approach to governance.

The Thermidorians also took steps to **restore social order and personal freedoms**. During the Terror, citizens had lived under constant surveillance, with neighborhood watch committees empowered to monitor and report any behavior deemed suspicious or counter-revolutionary. These committees, which had fostered a climate of paranoia and distrust, were gradually dissolved. This reform allowed citizens to regain a degree of privacy and freedom in their daily lives, ending the practice of forced conformity to revolutionary norms. By dismantling these surveillance networks, the Thermidorians signaled an end to the obsessive scrutiny that had permeated French society, reassuring the public that personal freedom was once again valued.

Politically, the Thermidorians pursued **institutional reforms** to prevent the concentration of power that had enabled the Committee of Public Safety's dominance. In 1795, they drafted the **Constitution of the Year III**, which established the **Directory**, a new executive body composed of five members. The Directory was designed to distribute power among several leaders rather than vest it in a single committee or individual. By creating a more balanced system, the Thermidorians hoped to avoid the authoritarianism that had marked the Terror and to stabilize the Republic with a framework of checks and balances. The new constitution also limited voting rights to property-owning men, marking a conservative turn in revolutionary ideals and signaling a shift away from the radical democracy of the past.

The Thermidorians aimed to **restore public confidence in the Revolution** by emphasizing a return to stability, moderation, and pragmatic governance. They actively distanced themselves from the rhetoric of virtue and purity that had characterized Robespierre's rule, focusing instead on rebuilding the economy, stabilizing social conditions, and ensuring that citizens could live without fear of repression. This reaction against extremism helped to temper the Revolution, though it left many, especially the lower classes, disappointed with the limited scope of reform.

The **Thermidorian Reaction's reforms** thus marked a departure from the Revolution's earlier radicalism, redirecting it toward a more restrained and structured form of governance. While challenges persisted and discontent simmered, the Thermidorian policies effectively ended the culture of terror and reintroduced a measure of civil liberties. The Directory that emerged from these reforms, though flawed and often unstable, represented the Thermidorians' commitment to balancing revolutionary ideals with the practical need for order and stability.

Establishment of the Directory

The **Directory** was established in 1795 as a direct response to the chaos of the Reign of Terror and the absolutism of the Committee of Public Safety. Its creators sought to design a system that would prevent the concentration of power that had characterized the previous government. To achieve this, the Constitution of the Year III introduced a new form of governance with a **separation of powers**, balancing authority between the executive and the legislature. The executive body, known as the Directory, consisted of five members chosen by the legislature, each holding office for five years on a staggered basis, with one member replaced each year. This design aimed to ensure continuity while avoiding the autocratic tendencies that had brought the Revolution to the brink of collapse.

The Directory worked alongside a **bicameral legislature**, a system inspired by previous revolutionary efforts to create a more representative government. The legislature was split into two chambers: the Council of Five Hundred, which proposed legislation, and the Council of Ancients, which reviewed and approved or rejected these proposals. The separation of the legislative and executive functions created a system of checks and balances intended to curb the possibility of any one faction or leader gaining too much influence. This structure was markedly conservative compared to the radical democracy of the earlier revolutionary governments, reflecting the Thermidorians' desire for stability over ideological purity.

The Directory also introduced **voting restrictions** that limited political participation to property-owning men, a move that distanced the government from the more inclusive ideals of 1792. This restriction aimed to reduce the influence of the sans-culottes and the Parisian radicals, whom the Thermidorians blamed for much of the violence and disorder of the Terror. By excluding the urban poor from direct political power, the Directory hoped to align governance with the interests of the middle and upper classes, whom it saw as more invested in maintaining order. However, this limitation also alienated a significant portion of the population, who felt increasingly disconnected from the political process.

Economically, the Directory tried to stabilize France by introducing **currency reforms** and addressing inflation, a lingering issue that had plagued the revolutionary economy. The previous currency, the assignat, had been rendered nearly worthless due to over-issuance, leading to rampant inflation and economic hardship. The Directory replaced the assignat with the mandate, a new currency designed to restore confidence in the economy. However, this measure met with limited success, as economic instability continued to challenge the government's authority. The Directory's currency reforms reflected its emphasis on pragmatic solutions over revolutionary zeal, though they often failed to achieve the intended outcomes.

Despite its conservative foundations, the Directory faced **internal factionalism** from the start. The executive structure made it difficult for any single leader to establish dominance, yet it also fostered internal competition and power struggles. Each director pursued their own political alliances, often resulting in conflicts that weakened the government's effectiveness. The Directory's dependence on the military to suppress uprisings and maintain control further complicated its position. As a result, France's generals, especially young and ambitious leaders like Napoleon Bonaparte, gained significant influence within the government, foreshadowing the military's role in shaping the nation's future.

Challenges Facing the New Government

From its inception, the Directory faced **major challenges** that undermined its ability to govern effectively. One of the primary issues was the **ongoing economic crisis**. Inflation continued to strain the economy, as prices for basic goods remained high and wages failed to keep up. The Directory's attempts to stabilize the currency with the mandate were unsuccessful, as public confidence in paper money was virtually nonexistent after the collapse of the assignat. Many citizens, particularly in the working class, suffered from high prices, food shortages, and unemployment, leading to increased resentment against the government. The economic difficulties fueled social unrest, as people questioned whether the Directory was capable of providing the stability and prosperity they had hoped for after the Terror.

The **political divisions within the legislature** also made governance difficult. The Council of Five Hundred and the Council of Ancients were split between moderates and more radical or royalist factions, creating an environment of constant ideological struggle. The Directory's executive members often found themselves pulled in different directions as they attempted to appease both sides. Royalists, who hoped to restore the monarchy, began to gain influence, while Jacobin remnants pushed for a return to the more democratic and egalitarian values of the early Revolution. This internal conflict made it nearly impossible for the Directory to implement cohesive policies, as it was forced to navigate a complex web of competing interests and shifting alliances.

Externally, the Directory faced **military pressures** from ongoing wars with European powers. The Revolutionary Wars, which had begun under the National Convention, continued to demand extensive resources and manpower. Although French forces achieved significant victories under generals like Napoleon Bonaparte, the wars drained the government's finances and led to widespread war-weariness among the public. The military campaigns provided a temporary distraction from domestic issues, but they also kept France in a state of perpetual mobilization. The reliance on military success to uphold national morale put enormous pressure on the Directory to secure constant victories, creating a situation where military leaders, especially Napoleon, began to wield more influence over political affairs.

The **Directory's dependence on the army** to maintain internal order further destabilized its authority. Domestic unrest, particularly in regions where support for the monarchy or the Church remained strong, required frequent military intervention. The Vendée and other areas that had resisted the Revolution continued to pose threats to the government's control, necessitating the use of force to suppress uprisings. This dependence on the military empowered generals, who were often more popular with the people than the Directory itself. The army's increasing political clout made it difficult for the Directory to assert civilian authority, as it became clear that its survival depended heavily on the loyalty of military leaders.

Popular discontent with the Directory grew as its **economic policies disproportionately benefited the wealthy**. The government's removal of price controls allowed prices to rise, affecting the working class most severely, while wealthier citizens benefited from a freer market. This approach aligned with the Directory's conservative outlook but deepened the divide between the classes. The sans-culottes and other lower-class citizens, who had once driven revolutionary fervor, felt abandoned by the government. Their dissatisfaction sparked occasional protests and uprisings, although these were quickly suppressed. Nonetheless, the tension between the Directory's policies and the expectations of the common people created a climate of widespread disillusionment and frustration.

The Directory also faced **corruption scandals** that further eroded public trust. Many directors and officials engaged in bribery, embezzlement, and other corrupt practices, exploiting their positions for personal gain. The government's perceived corruption fed into the growing sense that the Revolution's ideals had been betrayed. Instead of the equality and justice promised at the Revolution's outset, citizens saw a government increasingly concerned with maintaining power and privilege. This disillusionment became a significant factor in the Directory's loss of legitimacy, as people questioned whether the government represented their interests.

Perhaps the greatest challenge to the Directory was **Napoleon Bonaparte's rising influence**. As a successful general with widespread popular support, Napoleon's fame grew with each military victory, making him a potential threat to the Directory's authority. His Italian campaign brought him substantial acclaim and resources, and he became known as a hero of the Revolution. The Directory's reliance on Napoleon highlighted its own weakness, as it was clear that he held the loyalty of the army and the public's admiration. By 1799, his power had grown to the point where he could overthrow the government with relative ease, leading to the **coup of 18 Brumaire** and the establishment of the Consulate, which ended the Directory and the Revolution's final phase.

CHAPTER 15: THE RISE OF NAPOLEON AND THE END OF THE REVOLUTION

Military Success and Popularity of Napoleon

Napoleon Bonaparte's meteoric rise during the French Revolution was built on his **impressive military success and his popularity among the French people**, both of which ultimately propelled him to power and marked the end of the revolutionary period. Napoleon's career began modestly, but he quickly distinguished himself through bold strategies and a unique ability to inspire his troops. His victories on the battlefield transformed him from a promising young officer into a national hero and, ultimately, a political leader.

Napoleon's first major success came with his **Italian campaign in 1796-97**, where he led the French army against the Austrian forces, who were trying to reclaim lost territories. Despite being outnumbered and dealing with limited supplies, Napoleon's innovative tactics turned the tide in France's favor. He famously led his troops through the challenging terrain of the Alps, surprising the Austrian forces with his speed and audacity. By dividing his army into smaller, more mobile units, he struck where the enemy least expected, defeating Austrian forces in a series of swift and decisive battles. Victories at **Arcole, Rivoli, and Lodi** demonstrated his skill as a commander and allowed France to secure its hold on northern Italy.

In addition to military success, **Napoleon's leadership style set him apart**. He spent time with his soldiers, shared in their hardships, and addressed them directly in stirring speeches that reinforced their sense of purpose. Soldiers admired him not only for his tactical skill but for his charisma. He often referred to his men as "comrades" and maintained a close connection with them, earning their loyalty and admiration. His troops saw him as a leader who genuinely cared about their well-being, which inspired a fierce loyalty that proved invaluable in battle. Napoleon's understanding of morale allowed him to turn exhausted, poorly supplied troops into an effective fighting force capable of defeating well-equipped enemies.

This **campaign in Italy not only secured Napoleon's military reputation** but also gave him political power. After defeating the Austrians, he negotiated the Treaty of Campo Formio, securing territory for France and establishing client states that would strengthen French influence in Europe. This treaty, negotiated without direct orders from the Directory, showed his willingness to act independently and proved his skill as both a soldier and a diplomat. The Directory, although wary of his growing influence, could not deny the value of his successes. By securing French dominance in Italy, Napoleon effectively shifted the power balance in Europe, undermining Austria's influence and demonstrating that France was still a force to be reckoned with.

The **Egyptian campaign of 1798-1799** further enhanced Napoleon's public image, even though it was ultimately a strategic failure. His goal was to weaken Britain by cutting off its trade routes to India, one of Britain's most valuable colonies. Napoleon won a stunning victory at the **Battle of the Pyramids**, where he used innovative square formations to protect his troops against the larger numbers of Mamluk cavalry. This victory allowed France to seize control of Cairo and establish a presence in Egypt, which was portrayed back in France as a heroic endeavor. However, the British navy, led by **Admiral Horatio Nelson**, defeated the French fleet at the **Battle of the Nile**, isolating Napoleon's army in Egypt.

Despite the setback in Egypt, **Napoleon's propaganda machine worked tirelessly** to maintain his image as a hero. Newspapers in France were filled with stories of his bravery and triumphs, often omitting or downplaying the more difficult aspects of the campaign. The French public viewed him as a bold and ambitious leader who represented the spirit of the Revolution, someone willing to challenge the great powers and extend France's influence. Napoleon's popularity surged, and many citizens began to see him as the only figure capable of restoring order and ensuring France's security.

Overthrow of the Directory

By 1799, the Directory had lost public support due to its corruption, inefficiency, and inability to stabilize France. Economic crises, ongoing wars, and internal divisions left it deeply unpopular and vulnerable. For Napoleon and his allies, the Directory's weakness presented an opportunity to seize power and reshape the government. With a carefully orchestrated plan, Napoleon and his closest allies prepared to dismantle the Directory in a swift coup that would lead to the formation of the Consulate.

Napoleon had returned from his campaign in Egypt earlier in October 1799. Although his army had remained stranded after the British defeat at the Battle of the Nile, he still returned as a celebrated hero, largely due to the propaganda that painted his campaign as a triumph. With widespread disillusionment over the Directory's governance, Napoleon's arrival in Paris ignited hope among citizens who saw him as a symbol of strength and order. Napoleon capitalized on his popularity, aligning himself with key figures like **Emmanuel Sieyès**, a prominent political thinker and one of the Directory's directors, who had also grown critical of the government. Sieyès had already devised a plan to replace the Directory with a stronger executive but lacked the military support to execute it alone. Recognizing Napoleon's popularity and military backing, Sieyès found in him a perfect partner for the coup.

On the morning of **18 Brumaire**, the plan began to unfold. Sieyès, along with Napoleon's brother Lucien, who was the President of the Council of Five Hundred, convinced the Directory to convene the legislative councils at the

Château de Saint-Cloud, outside Paris, under the pretext of an alleged Jacobin conspiracy that required urgent action. The relocation served a strategic purpose, allowing Napoleon to secure the Parisian streets with loyal troops while removing the council from the political hotbed of the capital. The maneuver effectively isolated the councils, placing them at Napoleon's mercy while creating an illusion of an imminent threat to France that justified military intervention.

At Saint-Cloud, tensions were high, and the coup quickly encountered resistance. The **Council of Five Hundred**—the lower house of the legislature—was particularly resistant, with members calling out Napoleon as a tyrant attempting to usurp power. Recognizing the risk of losing control, Lucien Bonaparte intervened, defending Napoleon and urging the council members to support the proposed reforms. Yet, the opposition grew vocal, and cries of "Outlaw him!" echoed through the chamber. At this critical moment, Lucien ordered Napoleon's soldiers to enter the chamber, dispersing the deputies by force. Amidst the chaos, Lucien claimed that extremists within the council had attempted to assassinate his brother, portraying the coup as a necessary action to protect the state from internal threats.

With the Council of Five Hundred subdued, Napoleon and his allies faced the **Council of Ancients**, the upper house, which was more amenable to their plans. The Ancients quickly approved a motion to dissolve the Directory, giving Napoleon and Sieyès the legal cover they needed to declare the government defunct. By the end of the day, the Directory was formally abolished, and a new provisional government, the Consulate, was proclaimed. Although Sieyès had initially intended the Consulate to be a shared executive among three men, it became clear that Napoleon had no intention of sharing power equally. His military command and popularity with the public allowed him to dominate the new structure, positioning himself as the clear leader.

The **overthrow of the Directory** was executed with remarkable speed, leveraging military presence, political maneuvering, and the illusion of imminent threat. The coup was carefully framed to appear as a defensive measure, appealing to a population tired of political instability and desperate for strong leadership. For the French people, the end of the Directory was a relief, as the government's corruption, internal conflicts, and lack of vision had failed to address France's pressing needs. The Revolution, which had once promised liberty and equality, had devolved into years of turmoil, leaving citizens disillusioned. Napoleon's promise of order, stability, and renewed national glory resonated with many who hoped his leadership would bring the peace and direction that had been missing.

Establishment of the Consulate and End of Revolutionary France

Following the Directory's collapse, **Napoleon established the Consulate**, a new government that marked the end of revolutionary France and the beginning of an authoritarian regime under his rule. The Consulate was structured to provide France with strong central leadership while ostensibly maintaining republican principles. However, its design concentrated power heavily in the hands of the First Consul—Napoleon himself. Alongside him were two additional consuls, Sieyès and Roger Ducos, though their roles were largely symbolic. The structure of the Consulate made it clear from the outset that Napoleon intended to shape France's political future in his image, asserting control over both the executive and legislative branches.

The Consulate's formation was formalized with the **Constitution of the Year VIII**, drafted largely by Sieyès but modified significantly by Napoleon to suit his ambitions. The constitution established a complex system of indirect elections, where voters selected "notables," who then chose representatives to serve in the legislature. This system was designed to limit popular influence, ensuring that political power remained concentrated among the elite while giving an appearance of democratic participation. The real power rested with the First Consul, who held control over the army, foreign policy, and most domestic matters. In practice, this constitution sidelined the legislature and centralized authority in Napoleon's hands, enabling him to govern with minimal opposition.

Napoleon's **policies during the Consulate reflected his vision for a stable, unified France**. One of his first actions was to consolidate his support among the military and the bourgeoisie, groups he saw as essential to maintaining his authority. He improved soldiers' conditions and promised wealth and advancement to officers loyal to his regime. For the bourgeoisie, Napoleon offered stability and protection of property rights, ensuring their support in exchange for their influence and resources. This approach garnered loyalty from both the military and the middle class, securing Napoleon's foundation of power. His policies focused on stability, promising to end the chaos that had plagued France under the previous governments.

The Consulate brought sweeping **reforms to France's legal and administrative systems**. Napoleon's most famous contribution, the **Napoleonic Code**, laid the foundation for modern French civil law. The code codified principles of property rights, individual liberties, and equality before the law while preserving traditional values around family and authority. It standardized legal practices across France, replacing the complex patchwork of local laws that had existed under the Ancien Régime. The Napoleonic Code embodied the Enlightenment ideals of rationality and order but with an authoritarian bent, as it centralized judicial authority and restricted certain freedoms, such as press and political assembly, to prevent dissent.

Additionally, Napoleon reformed France's **educational system**, establishing lycées to train future administrators and military officers. These state-run schools focused on discipline, loyalty, and civic responsibility, cultivating a new generation of citizens loyal to the Consulate. By shaping the education system to serve the state's needs, Napoleon ensured that his vision would influence future generations. Education became a tool of the state, aligning with his broader strategy of instilling a sense of national unity and loyalty that transcended the revolutionary ideals of individual freedom.

The Consulate also addressed the **long-standing divide between Church and state**, a source of conflict throughout the Revolution. In 1801, Napoleon signed the **Concordat with Pope Pius VII**, reestablishing Catholicism's presence in France while maintaining control over the Church's operations. The Concordat allowed the Church to regain some of its former authority but under the supervision of the state. Napoleon's pragmatic approach to religion reflected his desire to appease both traditionalists and revolutionaries, aiming to unite French society under a single government without alienating either side.

Although the Consulate's policies sought to reconcile revolutionary ideals with stability, the government itself marked the **end of revolutionary France**. The Consulate embodied a new form of authoritarian rule under Napoleon's direct control, moving away from the republicanism that had defined earlier phases of the Revolution. The revolutionary pursuit of liberty, equality, and fraternity gave way to centralized authority, national unity, and the pursuit of empire. As First Consul, Napoleon wielded power similar to that of a monarch, though he framed his rule as a continuation of revolutionary progress. Within a few years, he would declare himself Emperor, solidifying his personal rule and signaling that the Revolution, as it had once been envisioned, was over.

CHAPTER 16: LEGACY OF THE FRENCH REVOLUTION

Social and Political Impact on France

The **French Revolution's social and political impact** on France was profound, marking a transformation that reached nearly every part of society and reshaped the country's identity. The Revolution's legacy continued to influence France well after its end, embedding ideals like equality, citizenship, and secular governance into the national consciousness. Although the path to these goals was tumultuous, the Revolution initiated a shift from a society dominated by monarchy, nobility, and the Church to one that, at least in principle, valued individual rights, meritocracy, and representative governance.

One of the Revolution's most striking social impacts was the **abolition of feudal privileges**. Under the Ancien Régime, French society was structured in three estates, where the clergy and nobility enjoyed extensive privileges, exempt from many taxes and often owning vast tracts of land. The Third Estate—comprised of commoners, peasants, and the working class—bore the burden of taxes and had limited political power. With the Revolution, this structure was dismantled, beginning with the **August Decrees of 1789**, which eliminated feudal dues and privileges. Peasants no longer had to pay seigneurial dues, and many hereditary privileges were abolished. This sweeping change altered rural life, giving former peasants a sense of autonomy and contributing to the breakdown of the old, rigid social hierarchy.

The **Declaration of the Rights of Man and of the Citizen** in 1789 further codified these new principles, affirming that all men were born free and equal in rights. This document became a foundation for the revolutionary government and remains a powerful symbol in French culture. It declared rights to liberty, property, security, and resistance to oppression, setting a new standard for governance. Although these ideals were not consistently applied throughout the Revolution, they marked a radical departure from the past and provided a blueprint for future generations. These concepts of citizenship and equality would later be echoed in French constitutions and embedded in the fabric of French society.

The Revolution's impact extended to **education and civic engagement**. The revolutionary government saw an educated populace as essential to the new Republic, aiming to foster a sense of civic responsibility among citizens. Reforms laid the groundwork for a more accessible education system, though implementation varied. Schooling became associated with national values and the idea of producing informed citizens rather than simply subjects of the crown. While comprehensive, state-run education would take time to establish, the Revolution started a movement that emphasized education as a tool for enlightenment and civic unity, a view that shaped later French policy.

One of the most enduring social changes was the **decline of the Church's authority**. Before the Revolution, the Catholic Church held immense power in French society, owning a significant portion of land and influencing political decisions. The Revolution's secular ideals challenged this power, beginning with the **Civil Constitution of the Clergy** in 1790, which placed the Church under state control and required clergy to swear loyalty to the state over the Pope. Later, the radical phase of the Revolution brought about dechristianization efforts, closing churches, banning religious symbols, and replacing them with festivals celebrating revolutionary ideals. Although Napoleon would later reconcile with the Church through the Concordat of 1801, the Church never regained its former authority. The Revolution laid the foundation for a secular state where religion and governance were separate, a principle that remains central in French politics today.

In terms of political impact, the Revolution introduced the **concept of popular sovereignty**—the idea that authority derives from the people, not divine right or hereditary privilege. This principle reshaped French governance and inspired demands for representation, leading to the creation of the National Assembly and later the National Convention. Although France experienced numerous regime changes in the years that followed, from the Consulate to the Empire to the restoration of the monarchy, the idea that the government should represent the people endured. The Revolution ended the monarchy's unquestioned power and made France a nation where political legitimacy depended on the people's will, a shift that would continue to influence French politics.

The **rise of political clubs** and increased public participation in governance also changed the political landscape. Clubs like the Jacobins and Cordeliers fostered political debate and offered citizens a way to participate in the Revolution beyond voting, engaging with ideas and taking direct action. Although the Jacobins and other clubs were later suppressed, the culture of political engagement they created did not vanish. It set a precedent for organized political expression that continued into the 19th century and beyond, as groups across the political spectrum continued to form associations, promote their causes, and influence public opinion. The Revolution encouraged a participatory model where ordinary citizens felt empowered to question and shape their government.

The **legal reforms of the Napoleonic era** were deeply influenced by revolutionary ideals, particularly the creation of the **Napoleonic Code** in 1804. This civil code standardized laws across France, reflecting the Revolution's principles of equality before the law, property rights, and the rejection of feudal privileges. By simplifying legal practices and removing privileges based on birth, the Napoleonic Code became a lasting legacy, both in France and in countries influenced by French administration during Napoleon's conquests. Even after Napoleon's fall, the Code's principles endured, helping to create a sense of legal equality and fairness that would shape French society for generations.

The Revolution's impact on **women's rights and social roles** was complex and mixed. While women participated actively in the Revolution, organizing protests like the **Women's March on Versailles** and forming political clubs, they did not achieve full legal equality. Initially, revolutionary leaders like Olympe de Gouges championed women's rights, as seen in her **Declaration of the Rights of Woman and the Female Citizen**. However, as the Revolution progressed, women's political participation was restricted, and they were eventually barred from political clubs. The Napoleonic Code reinforced traditional gender roles, positioning women primarily as dependents within the family. Nonetheless, the Revolution set in motion discussions about women's rights and roles in society, sparking early feminist ideas that would resurface in later movements.

The Revolution also led to the **spread of nationalism** as a unifying force in French society. The revolutionary government promoted the idea of a common identity based on shared values, such as liberty, equality, and fraternity, rather than loyalty to a king or dynasty. National pride grew as citizens identified with the Republic and saw themselves as active participants in the nation's destiny. The revolutionary wars contributed to this sense of national unity, as French citizens rallied to defend their country from foreign monarchies attempting to restore the old order. This form of civic nationalism would shape French identity and influence other movements across Europe.

Although the Revolution's achievements were often inconsistent and met with setbacks, its **long-term impact on political and social life in France** cannot be understated. By dismantling feudal structures, affirming principles of citizenship, promoting secular governance, and introducing representative ideals, the Revolution redefined what it meant to be a citizen in France. It replaced the old hierarchical system with one based, at least in principle, on merit and equality, laying the groundwork for modern French society.

Influence on Global Revolutionary Movements

The **French Revolution's influence on global revolutionary movements** was vast, reaching far beyond France's borders to inspire uprisings, independence movements, and social reforms worldwide. Its ideals of liberty, equality, and fraternity, enshrined in the Declaration of the Rights of Man and of the Citizen, resonated deeply with people living under oppressive regimes, sparking a wave of revolutions and social change across Europe, the Americas, and beyond. The Revolution showed that entrenched systems of monarchy and aristocratic privilege could be challenged, a notion that inspired those who sought freedom and representation in their own countries.

One of the earliest and most notable global impacts was seen in **Haiti**, then a French colony known as Saint-Domingue. Inspired by the French Revolution's principles, enslaved and free Black people in Saint-Domingue launched a revolt in 1791, led by figures like **Toussaint L'Ouverture**. They demanded freedom and equality, echoing the revolutionary rhetoric of France. The Haitian Revolution, which resulted in Haiti's independence in 1804, was the first successful slave rebellion in history and created the first Black republic. Although Haiti's independence was met with resistance from global powers, the Haitian Revolution demonstrated the power of revolutionary ideals to inspire resistance against oppression, setting a precedent for anti-colonial and anti-slavery movements in the Americas and beyond.

In **Latin America**, the French Revolution's example provided both a model and a catalyst for independence movements. Leaders like **Simón Bolívar** and **José de San Martín** drew on the principles of self-determination and equality as they led independence struggles against Spanish colonial rule. Bolívar, influenced by Enlightenment ideas and the events in France, envisioned a unified, free Latin America where citizens held power rather than European monarchs. His campaigns led to the liberation of several South American countries, including Venezuela, Colombia, and Bolivia. Although the political realities in Latin America differed from France, the Revolution's legacy helped forge a movement that challenged colonial control and sought national sovereignty.

The French Revolution's influence extended into **Europe**, especially during the Napoleonic Wars. As French armies spread revolutionary ideals across the continent, they disrupted feudal and monarchical systems, bringing about social and political changes in many regions. In places like Italy, Germany, and the Netherlands, Napoleonic forces abolished feudal privileges, established legal reforms, and promoted the idea of equal citizenship. While many European monarchs resisted these changes, the principles introduced during the Revolution remained embedded in these societies, fueling later nationalist and liberal movements. The Revolution's legacy planted the seeds for the **European Revolutions of 1848**, a series of uprisings aimed at expanding political representation and implementing social reforms. Although these revolutions were largely suppressed, they demonstrated the enduring appeal of revolutionary ideals, setting the stage for future democratic developments across the continent.

In the **United States**, the French Revolution reaffirmed and expanded upon the ideals of the American Revolution, particularly in its emphasis on equality and popular sovereignty. Many Americans viewed the French Revolution as a continuation of their own struggle for freedom, and figures like **Thomas Jefferson** expressed support for the events in France. The radical phase of the French Revolution, however, created tensions, with Federalists like **Alexander Hamilton** opposing the violence associated with the Reign of Terror. Nevertheless, the Revolution's early ideals influenced American politics, contributing to debates about democracy, rights, and the limits of government. The French Revolution helped shape American identity, showing that revolutionary ideals could evolve and spark dialogue in countries already established as republics.

In **Asia and Africa**, the French Revolution's influence emerged gradually, primarily through the experiences of colonial subjects who witnessed or learned about the upheavals in Europe. As European empires expanded, many colonized people began to question the legitimacy of foreign rule. In **India**, leaders like **Tipu Sultan** resisted British colonialism, drawing inspiration from the revolutionary spirit of resistance against oppression. Similarly, intellectuals and activists in the 19th century who sought independence from European powers often invoked the Revolution's principles. Although revolutionary movements in these regions gained momentum later, the ideas of equality, national sovereignty, and self-rule began to take root during the revolutionary era, providing a foundation for the anti-colonial struggles of the 20th century.

The **French Revolution's cultural and intellectual legacy** spread globally through literature, political thought, and social activism. Writers and thinkers such as **Mary Wollstonecraft** and **Thomas Paine** were deeply influenced by the Revolution, advocating for rights and social reforms in their own contexts. Wollstonecraft, inspired by revolutionary ideals, wrote **A Vindication of the Rights of Woman**, challenging traditional gender roles and calling for women's equality. Her work laid an early foundation for feminist thought, showing how the Revolution's principles could be applied beyond political governance to address social inequalities. Paine, who had supported both the American and French Revolutions, emphasized universal rights and the power of the people, helping to spread these ideas to audiences in England and America.

In **China and Japan**, 19th-century intellectuals viewed the French Revolution as a model for modernization and reform. Japanese thinkers in the **Meiji period** studied European revolutionary ideas as they sought to transform Japan into a powerful, modern nation. China's **May Fourth Movement** in 1919, which protested foreign influence and called for reform, also echoed revolutionary principles of self-determination and social justice, showing the Revolution's indirect but lasting impact in Asia. These movements adapted French revolutionary ideals to local contexts, underscoring the Revolution's broad applicability and enduring relevance in diverse cultural and political settings.

Lasting Effects on Modern Ideals of Equality, Rights, and Governance

The French Revolution **cemented foundational ideals** of equality, rights, and governance that have continued to shape modern societies. It challenged traditional hierarchies and asserted that all citizens were equal before the law—a principle enshrined in the **Declaration of the Rights of Man and of the Citizen**. This idea redefined relationships between individuals and the state, emphasizing that government existed to serve its people rather than to maintain the privileges of a select few. Today, the concept of equal rights remains central to modern democracies, reflecting the Revolution's commitment to dismantling systems of inherited privilege.

One of the Revolution's most enduring legacies is the **principle of popular sovereignty**. By establishing that political authority derived from the people, not from divine right or hereditary rule, the Revolution inspired the democratic movements that followed. This shift laid the groundwork for representative governance, where citizens hold the right to choose their leaders and influence political decisions. Popular sovereignty also fostered the concept of **constitutionalism**, as seen in the various constitutions drafted during the Revolution. Although many of these constitutions were short-lived, they demonstrated the revolutionary belief in a written framework to limit power and protect citizens' rights. This emphasis on constitutional law remains a cornerstone of modern democracies.

The Revolution's impact on **legal equality** can be seen in the development of the **Napoleonic Code**, which enshrined the principle of equality before the law and abolished feudal privileges. The Code's influence spread beyond France, shaping legal systems across Europe and in countries as far-reaching as Latin America and Canada. By emphasizing secular, rational legal principles, the Napoleonic Code helped to institutionalize equality and the rule of law, values that continue to define modern legal systems. Even today, many aspects of civil law globally are based on or influenced by this code, illustrating the Revolution's role in standardizing the legal protections citizens expect from their governments.

In the realm of **individual rights**, the French Revolution advanced the idea that every citizen was entitled to basic liberties. The Declaration of the Rights of Man emphasized freedom of speech, press, and religion, rights that are now considered fundamental in democratic societies. Although the Revolution itself did not always uphold these freedoms, especially during the Reign of Terror, its ideals influenced subsequent generations. Many countries incorporated similar rights into their constitutions, recognizing them as essential to personal autonomy and democratic participation. The revolutionary notion that these rights were universal, applying to all people rather than a privileged few, set a global standard that continues to resonate.

The Revolution's **commitment to secularism** reshaped governance by asserting that the state should remain neutral in religious matters. This secular approach was initially enforced through the **Civil Constitution of the Clergy** and later reinforced by efforts to separate church and state. The idea that religion should not interfere with politics became central to French society, and this secular model influenced countries worldwide, particularly as secularism grew in 19th- and 20th-century governance. Modern secular states continue to reflect this legacy, balancing freedom of religion with a commitment to prevent religious influence in political affairs.

Finally, the Revolution emphasized **social justice and civic duty**, urging citizens to contribute to the common good. The concepts of fraternity and civic responsibility introduced by the Revolution have shaped the idea of an engaged citizenry that actively participates in shaping society. This sense of civic duty inspired movements for social reform, welfare policies, and public education, reinforcing the idea that governments should address not only individual rights but also collective well-being. The Revolution's legacy in promoting these values remains alive in modern concepts of citizenship, human rights, and equality.

CHAPTER 17: TIMELINE AND TERMS

Timeline

Here is a **timeline of the French Revolution**, covering the key events from the initial seeds of discontent to the long-term legacy and aftermath of the Revolution. This will capture the major developments, figures, and transitions that marked each stage of the Revolution's course.

Prelude to Revolution: Seeds of Discontent (1780s)

Economic Strains and Financial Crisis
- **1780s**: France faces a severe financial crisis due to costly wars (including the American War of Independence), poor harvests, and rising national debt. Heavy taxation on the Third Estate (commoners) creates resentment.

Social Inequality and the Estates System
- French society is divided into three estates: the clergy (First Estate), the nobility (Second Estate), and the commoners (Third Estate). Only the Third Estate pays significant taxes, while the nobility and clergy enjoy privileges.

Enlightenment Ideals
- Philosophers like Rousseau, Voltaire, and Montesquieu inspire demands for equality, individual rights, and the limitation of monarchy.

Influence of the American Revolution (1775–1783)
- France's support for American independence demonstrates the possibility of overthrowing oppressive rule, and returning soldiers bring revolutionary ideals back to France.

1789: The Revolution Begins

May 5 – The Estates-General Convened
- For the first time since 1614, King Louis XVI calls the Estates-General, a gathering of representatives from all three estates, to address the financial crisis. However, voting procedures are biased toward the nobility and clergy, fueling Third Estate frustration.

June 17 – The Third Estate Declares the National Assembly
- Frustrated by their lack of influence, the Third Estate declares itself the National Assembly, claiming to represent the French people.

June 20 – The Tennis Court Oath

- Locked out of their usual meeting hall, National Assembly members take the Tennis Court Oath, vowing not to disband until they create a new constitution for France.

July 14 – The Storming of the Bastille
- Parisian citizens storm the Bastille prison, a symbol of royal tyranny, in response to rumors of a royal crackdown on the National Assembly. This marks the first violent act of the Revolution and is celebrated as a national holiday in France.

August 4 – Abolition of Feudal Privileges
- The National Assembly abolishes feudal privileges and seigneurial rights, eliminating the noble and clerical privileges and effectively ending feudalism.

August 26 – Declaration of the Rights of Man and of the Citizen
- Inspired by Enlightenment ideals, this declaration enshrines individual rights, equality before the law, and sovereignty of the people.

1790: Consolidating Revolutionary Gains

July 12 – Civil Constitution of the Clergy
- The National Assembly enacts the Civil Constitution, which places the Church under state control and requires clergy to swear allegiance to the state. This divides the country and alienates devout Catholics.

Women's March on Versailles (October 5–6, 1789)
- Driven by hunger and economic hardship, Parisian women march to Versailles, demanding action from the king. They force the royal family to move to the Tuileries Palace in Paris, making them virtual prisoners of the Revolution.

1791: France Moves Toward a Constitutional Monarchy

June 20–21 – King's Flight to Varennes
- King Louis XVI and his family attempt to escape to Austria but are captured at Varennes and returned to Paris. This event deepens mistrust between the king and revolutionaries, fueling calls for a republic.

September 3 – France's First Constitution
- The National Assembly adopts the Constitution of 1791, creating a constitutional monarchy with limited royal powers and a unicameral legislature. However, tensions between monarchists and republicans continue to grow.

1792: The Radical Revolution and the End of Monarchy

April 20 – War with Austria
- France declares war on Austria, believing the conflict will unite the nation and secure the Revolution from external threats. Prussia soon joins Austria, and the war goes poorly for France.

August 10 – Storming of the Tuileries Palace
- Revolutionary forces storm the Tuileries, capturing the king and declaring the monarchy suspended. This event marks the de facto end of the monarchy in France.

September 2–6 – September Massacres
- Amid fears of royalist plots, mobs massacre hundreds of suspected counter-revolutionaries in Parisian prisons. The violence reflects the Revolution's radical turn.

September 21 – France Declares a Republic
- The National Convention, newly elected to replace the Legislative Assembly, abolishes the monarchy and declares France a republic.

1793: The Reign of Terror Begins

January 21 – Execution of Louis XVI
- King Louis XVI is tried and convicted of treason. His execution by guillotine shocks Europe and solidifies the shift from monarchy to republic.

March – Committee of Public Safety Established
- The Convention establishes the Committee of Public Safety to protect the Revolution from internal and external threats, marking the start of centralized and authoritarian rule.

April 6 – Committee of Public Safety Takes Control
- Under leaders like **Maximilien Robespierre**, the Committee assumes nearly dictatorial powers, including control over the army and tribunals.

June 2 – Arrest of the Girondins
- The Girondins, a moderate faction, are purged from the Convention. The Jacobins, under Robespierre, now dominate the government, intensifying the Revolution's radical phase.

September 5 – Reign of Terror Officially Begins
- The government begins the systematic persecution of perceived enemies, leading to thousands of executions by guillotine. Revolutionary tribunals convict suspected counter-revolutionaries, and the Law of Suspects broadens the scope of arrests.

1794: The End of the Reign of Terror

June 10 – Law of 22 Prairial
- This law intensifies the Terror by allowing tribunals to convict suspects without substantial evidence, accelerating the rate of executions.

July 28 – Execution of Robespierre
- Robespierre and his allies are arrested and executed in a swift turnaround, ending the Reign of Terror. His death marks a shift back toward moderation in the Revolution.

1795–1799: The Thermidorian Reaction and the Directory Era

August 22, 1795 – Constitution of the Year III
- The Convention adopts a new constitution establishing the Directory, a five-man executive body, and a bicameral legislature. This conservative shift aims to stabilize France after the excesses of the Terror.

1795–1796 – Uprisings in the Vendée and Royalist Resistance
- The Directory faces numerous uprisings, including royalist and Jacobin challenges, but manages to maintain control, relying heavily on the military to suppress dissent.

1796–1797 – Napoleon's Italian Campaign
- Napoleon Bonaparte's military success in Italy enhances his reputation as a national hero. His victories secure territory and resources for France, increasing his influence.

1799: The Rise of Napoleon and the End of the Directory

November 9–10, 1799 (18 Brumaire) – Coup of 18 Brumaire
- Napoleon, with allies like Sieyès, overthrows the Directory in a coup, marking the end of the revolutionary government. The Consulate, with Napoleon as First Consul, is established, signaling a shift toward authoritarian rule.

1804: Napoleon Declares Himself Emperor

December 2, 1804 – Coronation of Napoleon
- Napoleon crowns himself Emperor of the French, formally ending the republican phase of the Revolution and ushering in the Napoleonic Empire. France is no longer a republic, and revolutionary ideals are subordinated to the consolidation of Napoleon's power.

Legacy and Aftermath of the Revolution (Post-1815)

1814–1815 – Fall of Napoleon and the Restoration of the Monarchy

- After Napoleon's defeat, the monarchy is briefly restored under Louis XVIII, although revolutionary ideals have permanently altered France.

Long-Term Impacts
- The Revolution's principles of equality, secularism, popular sovereignty, and human rights continue to influence French and global society. The Napoleonic Code, developed during Napoleon's rule, remains foundational to civil law in many countries.

Influence on Future Revolutions
- The Revolution's legacy inspires independence and social justice movements worldwide, including in Haiti, Latin America, and 19th-century Europe, where calls for representation, national sovereignty, and human rights echo France's revolutionary ideals.

Social and Political Transformation in France
- The Revolution permanently dismantled feudal privileges, established the concept of citizenship, and introduced republican governance, even if not consistently upheld. These changes shaped modern France, embedding the values of liberty, equality, and fraternity into its identity.

Terms and Definitions

- **Ancien Régime** – The political and social system in France before the Revolution, characterized by a monarchy and a rigid social hierarchy divided into three estates.
- **Estates-General** – An assembly representing the three estates (clergy, nobility, and commoners) called by the king in 1789 to address France's financial crisis, which led to the Revolution.
- **First Estate** – The clergy in pre-revolutionary France, who enjoyed privileges and were exempt from many taxes.
- **Second Estate** – The nobility in pre-revolutionary France, holding privileges like exemption from taxes and high-ranking positions.
- **Third Estate** – The commoners, including peasants, city workers, and the bourgeoisie, who carried the burden of taxation and lacked political influence before the Revolution.
- **Bourgeoisie** – The middle class in France, including merchants, professionals, and intellectuals, who sought more political power and were a driving force in the Revolution.
- **Tennis Court Oath** – A pledge taken by members of the Third Estate in 1789, vowing not to disband until they had created a new constitution for France.
- **National Assembly** – A revolutionary assembly formed by representatives of the Third Estate, which proclaimed itself the true representative body of the people.
- **Storming of the Bastille** – The attack on the Bastille prison on July 14, 1789, seen as the beginning of the Revolution and a symbol of revolt against tyranny.

- **Great Fear** – A period of panic and uprising in rural France during the summer of 1789, fueled by rumors of aristocratic plots.
- **August Decrees** – Laws passed in August 1789 by the National Assembly that abolished feudal privileges, ending the legal distinctions between estates.
- **Declaration of the Rights of Man and of the Citizen** – A document issued in 1789 asserting individual rights, equality before the law, and the sovereignty of the people.
- **Civil Constitution of the Clergy** – A law passed in 1790 that placed the Catholic Church under state control, requiring clergy to swear allegiance to the Revolution.
- **Women's March on Versailles** – A march by Parisian women to Versailles in October 1789, demanding bread and forcing the royal family to move to Paris.
- **Flight to Varennes** – The attempted escape by King Louis XVI and his family in June 1791, which ended in their capture and further eroded trust in the monarchy.
- **Constitution of 1791** – France's first constitution, which established a constitutional monarchy with limited powers for the king.
- **Sans-Culottes** – Radical working-class citizens of Paris who supported the Revolution and were instrumental in pushing it toward more radical phases.
- **Jacobin Club** – A political club of radical revolutionaries who supported the abolition of the monarchy and promoted a republican government.
- **Girondins** – A moderate revolutionary faction that favored a constitutional government and opposed the radical methods of the Jacobins.
- **Committee of Public Safety** – A powerful executive body established in 1793 to protect the Revolution, eventually leading the Reign of Terror.
- **Reign of Terror** – A period from 1793 to 1794 when the revolutionary government executed thousands of suspected enemies of the Revolution.
- **Maximilien Robespierre** – A leading figure of the Jacobins and the Committee of Public Safety, instrumental in the Reign of Terror until his own execution in 1794.
- **Law of Suspects** – A law passed in 1793 that broadened the definition of counter-revolutionaries, leading to mass arrests and executions.
- **Law of 22 Prairial** – A 1794 law that expedited the conviction and execution process for those accused of counter-revolutionary activities.
- **Cult of the Supreme Being** – A civic religion promoted by Robespierre in 1794 to replace Catholicism and unify citizens under a new moral order.
- **Thermidorian Reaction** – The reaction against the Reign of Terror that led to Robespierre's downfall in July 1794 and a shift toward moderation.
- **Directory** – The five-man executive body established in 1795, which governed France until Napoleon's coup in 1799.
- **Constitution of the Year III** – The 1795 constitution that established the Directory and a bicameral legislature, marking a conservative turn in the Revolution.
- **Coup of 18 Brumaire** – The 1799 coup in which Napoleon Bonaparte overthrew the Directory and established the Consulate, ending the Revolution.
- **Consulate** – The government established by Napoleon in 1799, with him as First Consul, marking the transition from revolution to authoritarian rule.

- **Napoleonic Code** – The civil code introduced by Napoleon in 1804, which standardized laws across France and enshrined principles of legal equality.
- **Louis XVI** – The king of France during the early stages of the Revolution, who was executed in 1793 after being convicted of treason.
- **Marie Antoinette** – The queen of France and wife of Louis XVI, who became a symbol of royal excess and was executed in 1793.
- **Republic of Virtue** – Robespierre's vision of a society based on revolutionary morals and civic virtue, promoted during the Reign of Terror.
- **Guillotine** – A device used for executions during the Revolution, symbolizing both justice and the violence of the Terror.
- **Feudalism** – The social and economic system of the Ancien Régime, characterized by hierarchical privileges and land-based wealth, abolished in 1789.
- **Secularism** – The principle of separating religious institutions from the government, established in France during the Revolution.
- **National Convention** – The assembly elected in 1792 that abolished the monarchy, declared France a republic, and guided the Revolution through its radical phase.
- **Declaration of Pillnitz** – A statement issued in 1791 by Austria and Prussia, declaring their intention to restore the French monarchy, which contributed to France's war with European powers.

AFTERWORD

As we reach the end of *French Revolution Step by Step*, I hope you've gained a deeper understanding of this remarkable period. The French Revolution was a time of sweeping change and powerful ideas, one that redefined not only a nation but the very concept of freedom, justice, and human rights. Taking this journey step by step, we've uncovered the roots, struggles, and triumphs of people who believed in the possibility of a better world.

Looking back, it's clear that the Revolution was far from perfect. It was a period filled with contradictions—calls for liberty clashing with acts of violence, and dreams of unity complicated by bitter divisions. The Revolution unleashed hope and horror in equal measure, challenging every person involved to consider what they were willing to sacrifice for the future they envisioned. For many, that meant risking—and sometimes losing—everything they had. From the peasants who revolted in rural France to the leaders in Paris who argued passionately for reform, their actions shaped the course of history and have continued to inspire movements for change around the world.

One of the great legacies of the Revolution is its powerful reminder of the human spirit's resilience. The people of France faced enormous odds, yet they believed that a fairer, freer society was worth fighting for. They sparked debates that still resonate today about equality, justice, and governance—debates that remind us that history is not just a record of the past but a conversation about what kind of future we want to create.

Today, as we reflect on the French Revolution, we can see its influence in the democratic ideals we often take for granted. The rights to vote, to speak freely, and to pursue equality are concepts that were fought for passionately in this era and that remain as relevant now as they were then. The Revolution taught us that progress is never straightforward or easy, but it's a journey worth undertaking.

I hope this book has provided you with a clearer picture of how a nation's struggle for change became a key moment in history. I hope, too, that it has shown how individuals, no matter their background, can contribute to something far greater than themselves. If nothing else, let the French Revolution remind us that our voices and actions matter and that change, while challenging, is possible when people come together with courage and determination.

Thank you for being part of this journey. As we close this book, may the lessons and stories from this incredible period continue to inspire you in the steps you take in your own life.

Printed in Great Britain
by Amazon